Salutations

BY THE SAME AUTHOR

Underwater Wedding (1961)
Sixpenny Poems (1962)
Well Ye Ken Noo (1963)
All Fall Down (1963)
The Worstest Beast (1965)
Penguin Modern Poets (1968)
The Grim Wayfarer (1969)
The Knitted Claymore (criticism) (1971)
Idiots Are Freelance (1973)
The Guardians Arrive (1978)
Star Child (1984)
To Stand Against The Wind (1985)
Heart of the Sun (1986)
Light Hearts (1987)

SALUTATIONS

Collected Poems 1960–1989

Alan Jackson

Polygon
EDINBURGH

First Published by
Polygon, 22 George Square,
Edinburgh

Typeset in Linotron Sabon
by Koinonia, Bury
Printed in Great Britain by
Bell and Bain Ltd, Glasgow

British Library Cataloguing in
Publication Data
Jackson, Alan, 1938–
Salutations: collected poems,
1960–1989.
I. Title
821'.914

ISBN 0 7486 6061 5
ISBN 0 7486 6033 X pbk

The publisher acknowledges
subsidy from the Scottish
Arts Council towards the
publication of this volume.

Preface

SINCE I was eighteen or so I have only had one purpose. I don't think it's mine alone but that it is laid into the foundation of the world, and in particular into the shape of this time. We are in combat for our spirit lives every second night and day; and I believe that what appears before us as history, society, politics etc are the outcome of how the individual millions are winning or losing in the struggle to understand and handle the giant forces that are active on and through the planet. This world-drama is now intensifying and deepening rapidly into colossal pressure upon persons to change, to understand or to become ill, disorientated, eventually far less than human.
We ourselves now are Antigone, Lear; Parsifal or Klingsor; Saul or Paul. There is a lot more to be said. Some of it is in the poems. *We shall meet at some dawn or some dusk.*

Alan Jackson
Edinburgh
August
1989

Acknowledgements

To the editors of the following magazine, collections, or anthologies: Akros, *All Fall Down* (The Kevin Press), The Anarchist, The Brown Bag, BBC Radios 1, 2, 3, and 4, BBC TV, Converse, Edinburgh Festival Poetry, Flame, Gambit, The Glasgow Herald, Impasto, Imprint, Lines, *Love Love Love* (Corgi), *Moderne Prosa und Lyrik der Britischen Inseln* (Aufbau Verlag), New North, New Saltire, *Penguin Modern Poets 12* (Penguin Press), The Scotsman, Scottish International, Sedna, Sonntag, and *The Worstest Beast* (Kevin Press), *The Old Pal's Act* (Allison and Busby), *Scottish Poetry 2, 3, 4, 5, 6,* (Edinburgh University Press), Aquarius, Teaching English, *Noise and Smokey Breath* (Third Eye Centre), *The Akros Anthology of Scottish Poetry* (65–70), *Contemporary Scottish Poetry* (Calder and Boyars), *A Touch of Flame* (Lion Publishing), *Transformation* (Rivelin Grapheme) and *Angels of Fire* (Chatto and Windus).

Contents

UNDERWATER WEDDING (1960–1961)

THE GRIM WAYFARER (1962–1969)

IDIOTS ARE FREELANCE (1963–1970)

THE GUARDIANS ARRIVE (1974–1976)

THE ATTIC POEMS (1976–1977)

UNDERWATER WEDDING

1960–1961

Curse you apples on that tree,
And curse our human destiny.
An ape, a bull, I'd rather be
Than civil suffering conscious me.

FOLLOW

Rather than not love, break.
For nothing less than wholeness make.
Forget the shatter you may shed;
Follow your feeling where it's been led.
Face the necessity, the knot
In which your younger selves are caught.
Make them free for where you're going:
The self includes all other knowing.
Morals and laws are unreal
Beside the struggle to get well.
The truest way of tackling evil
's loving marriage with the devil.

Everyone knows that heaven and hell
Don't outside us but inside dwell;
And so our wife and job as well:
Getting on after a lot of bother
With our ancient father-mother.

Don't be troubled by the men
Who'll ask you who and why and when.
You can't answer with a name
Till you and the asker are the same.
Man is more than time and place:
We're waiting for the human face.

DEVILS, ANGELS

Devils, angels, take my hand
And we'll make war on the human band.
Show them the use of energy is
To break the mould of centuries.

Endlessly their lives run on
While the pattern thins and the meaning fades,
And underneath there work and coil
Life's unlived lust and untried trades.

Show them that now
If to life they don't turn
An evil worm in their heart's dust
Will rage and burn.
All the malignancy
Of damned up potency
Will on their dishonest
Order burst,
And their machine society
Be forever
Crushed and curst.

*

Through forests and chasms of time I call,
Down history and through cities back
To when man was an animal
And walked in an unwedded track.

Give me power
And give me fire.
Give me freedom
And desire.
Give me stars
For hair,
Blossoms for
Body bare.
Give me back
My nose of smell,
My ear of hear.
My empty shell
Of manner, burn.
The being that
For mankind's sake,
And out of fear,
I bent and buckled –
Beat and turn
Back to the shape
For which I yearn.

Yet, Shape, I don't know your name
And that's my blame.
For free and wild I fought and
Now what to do and where –
I have forgotten.

*

I fear you refrigerator men,
With neon eyes in grey jobs,
With your down-kept life
Splitting off and sowing

Strange seeds inside you.
I fear the being you are paid
To conceal.
I fear black water
Collecting
Under tight roofs.

And you, schizophrenia,
Goddess of industrial society
Hard as shattered diamonds
Peopling the world with strange ghosts,
Things that were never meant to be.

DEATH

Naked as the bone
One has to be;
Naked as the winter,
Naked as the tree.

Till feeling flows
From deepest soul,
Must withhold
Feeling at all.

Wrong to involve
In what's corrupt.
Wrong to use others
To heal your cut.

Don't pretend;
Make no claim:
Strip to the bone
And grow again.

*

Sin's the spur behind creation.
Being becomes, for fears damnation.

*

The doom of name-bearing I
would gladly give back to the race,
to drown amongst the living and so
be rescued from upkeep of self.
What culture fought for I would fling away.
The higher you get it's cold,
And the winds don't reach, or the sea.

DRAMA

Fish are coupling
In my soul.
Male and female
Make one whole.

How I wish
I was there,
Underwater wedding
Of the dark and fair.

*

The double serpent winds me round
and I am lost and I am found.
I climb from earth into air
and back again: home nowhere.

*

Obscenities nest deep in my heart.
What a paradise for lost selves to play in.

*

Goodly godly kindly men,
If you pour I won't say when.

Wash me in the holy lather,
Ancient as my ancient father.

Scrub my toes eight nine ten,
Goodly godly kindly men.

*

Christ, unchristen me again.
Free me for the ancient men.

Holy water's not my need.
Best baptism is the seed.

Old sea and sun adorers knew
More than that spiritually biased Jew.

*

OUR FATHER

Gold of the flowering sun
Like an egg's been underdone
Flows into the world.
Heavenly chrysanthemum
Warms our bodies like good rum
Down our throats has trickled.

God divided into three,
Fire and flower and spirit be.

I'll love you if you'll love me.

*

Was a wee man
Who lived in an egg,
Sucked his own yolk,
Never did beg.

Sudden one morning

Set him yawning;
Stretched and stroke
Till the egg broke.

He ran into the world.
Air and earth skirled:
'Hooray, hurrah, he is free.
Gold and white and fighting is he.'

JANUARY

Deep dark hill beauties, women's eyes,
Peaks pools and depths, penalty and prize.
O birded
  unworded
  unflown
    –known
        soul,
How deep down? What horror? What filth
Nests in my heart-hole?

Hell is
Bird under water
Fish in sky.
Hell is descent into
Under the I.

Who turned my flower
Up-down?
Blossom in mud, roots in sky?

Beauty, beauty. Who stole my ring?
What whiskers claws come in between?

I am no man. Nowt.
I fling form from me like a foe
And neither swimming crawling walking go.
Womb or mould has not been made
In which my seed stuff may be laid.

An unkind hand threw back the gates
And the beasts came in.
        O my ancestors,
Who said I called? Crusty ones, bull,
Fin and wing, foot and pad,
Must I make room for you,
Human so long?
        Who ate my light,
I curse.
        Farewell, kind Mum and Dad,
The hairy ones have held me by the hand.

SAGE

if i were you
said the cod to the caterpillar
i'd have nothing to do
with circles or holes
they're all right
for them blind lads moles

for someone with spirit
there's no future in it

strike out on your own
be clean
be a bone

THE MONSTER FEELS THE HERO NEAR

Ha ha the light!
Bring to me.
Let me bite
and let me see.

I am the fish
dwells in deep seas,
the evil smeller
to make his heart freeze.

If he wants
there is escape.
Cut my kidneys,
make me gape.
And through the hole
the lad can leap.

*

A sea flowed in and filled my head;
I couldn't refuse to know.
It told me what to say and do
And showed me where to go.

When it drew back
It left myself
Enfeebled on the shore.
Distraught and strange I seemed
To those who laboured there.
I couldn't use the tools they used
Or wear the clothes they wore.

And I would walk in misery,
With neither friend or foe;
Waiting to hear the flash and surge
Of that swift self-drowning flow.

*

I am a body in which is demanding to be born
What the world isn't made for with its ordinary dawn.

Have I to go on throwing my humanity aside
To become to some terrible spirit the pained enchanted bride?

I am burning now already, my ashes in my hands.
I was not made to bear you that was made from common sands.

O help me, mother, O Earth, I'm being eaten daily
away
By the cruel desire for becoming of a being more
powerful than me.

*

Where have the angels of the change
gone?
Touched you with their wings and flew,
only once descending, only once, in need.
These holy high ones are meant to be unseen.
You brought them down to you.

Stop looking round to see if they'll come back,
bathing in the rosy. Forget their names.
Angels have their troubles too,
in other realms.

THE GRIM WAYFARER

1962–1969

contrary to the wind
i wake
in habits of mould and dust
for ingenuity
has its end in the dumps
and we quick heads
learn fear
of black reprisals

THE GRIM WAYFARER

Following the steepest path through the wood they came on the wild animals lapping and leaping in a clearing.

This whole matter must be cleared up to the satisfaction of the incumbent gods.

Declare your passport.

Slit! from his chest he drew a human heart.

And was greeted with the official clearance:

Go on. Leave that with us and pick it up when you return.

Swiftly he revised his plans. To go into the acroceranian mountains without a heart would be harder than he'd allowed for.

He grabbed a couple of leaves, squeezed them full of blood and tissue and shoved them into the cavity.

Should hold out till Jericho.

'All right, men! Let's march.'

The caravan of shambling idiots moved on into the waste.

On their right a mild glow pervaded. To their left the whiskers of mildew hung on the trees.

A low wind rose and tuffied their ankles and fluttered their rags so that from a distance they looked like a line of trees bending into the wind.

The hero led them with the confident stride of a man who knows not where he is going.

Whenever he consulted the map it said the same thing: Make for the black hump. Climb it and wait.

There was no black hump.

Muttering.

The hero didn't eat for forty fortnights and didn't notice that every two and a half days an old man died.

Finally he strode alone, whistling from somebody's Requiem and thinking of nothing.

When a black hump rose under his feet. There had been no climbing. But he was on top.

Was this a fulfilment of the map's directions or not?

He decided to wait.

A tree grew on the hump that shaded him from nothing.

Now, listen, it said. You are the grim wayfarer. You are no man's nothing. The end of tit. Hold out your pitcher and it will have the bottom broken. Knock, and the door will disappear. Seek, and you will be turned blind. This is my great news.

The tree shrank and the hump sank and he was left gently on the ground, weeping.

'Son, son,' a great voice boominated. 'Look up.'

Up! That was the last thing he had in mind.

Every one of his backbones creaked as he made the bend till his face was flat to the sky.

'See!'

And a flish flash of light out of the sky from east to west hung for a second and left a flame which floated and turned down to him. It was a babe.

'Take this child and press it between the leaves. Its blood and tissue are yours. It will mingle and grow. Don't be afraid. Nothing is foreign to flesh like yours.

You will wake up beside the frontier post. No guards now. They don't come out for the ones that come back. Don't stop for your old heart. Those who have it think they have you. Let them. They have catalogued and filed you. You are numbered and dead, as their counting goes. This is an asset. One of my best gifts though small.

Past the frontier you will be back in the world. I

have no advice. I know nothing about it. Except there is nothing unmasterable in it, though there is no end to its devilish re-arrangements.

Sing and walk light. And don't forget: the heart you hear pumping is an untouched charter. The other was too much countersigned by clerical devices.'

He walked back down the road past the sentries, standing in their coffins, and sang:

Tra la tra li la
I'll have wine for my breakfast
and pigskin for tea
I'll eat salt for supper,
start an inland sea.

O weary's the wearing
of ties made by men.
I'll use tomcats' tails
and the fruit of the hen.

On my forehead I'll paint
a badge of bright blue.
I'll throw off my old vest
and never buy new.

La di day day
scaramatoosh
I'll topple my lady
with a twinkle and push

And we will go riding
o'er but and o'er ben

and her legs and my legs
won't e'er part again.

So he whistled and jazzed
down the white april road
on his right hand a crow sat
and on his left hand a toad.

WHO SPAT

the black hatch
open the black hatch
hold in your teeth
the rose dark
take it
by the thorn
and kiss
the angels (to death)

the laughless
  danceless
  correcting angels
who spat
  on the coils of love

US OTHER GUYS

Man who used to swing from trees
and used his knees for shinning
now is master of the seas
and all that in em's swimming

Lions or elephants kept in cages
boggle the visitors' eyes:
buggered if I could've got him in there,
must have been some other guys.

Us other guys and our artefacts
are the human species,
who snuff and howl and dig and prowl
unconscious of our leashes.

Leashes the size of redwood trees
and light as a fish's bubble
hold on to us and walk us out
whistling, trouble, baby, trouble.

Trouble, trouble,
says fish on land,
says snake in flames,
says worm in hand.

But with gloves and goggles
homo mechanic
won't hear of concrete
turning volcanic.

*

Can the masters of desire be broken?
Can the terrible flames be killed
That charge wilfully through dark
Through day through all?
Can a set of complications be raised
That will keep matter down
And keep what matters moving?

LORD SAVE US. IT'S THE MINISTER

well Mr Mackay, ye're a bonny wee man
wi yer hat pulled down over yer balls
an yer lips so tight
nothing can pass through them
                                        bar silver

yer god's a triangular monster
    a sealed length of granite
if he touched a curve, he would crumble
                                                            and crash

get the hell off the surface of scotland
or i'll get the next bent moon
    to laugh you away in her tears.

THE LAST BAD

my heart beats fast against the last bad wall
feeds its force upon the thirteenth rib
evil serums push through all my blood
the cells enact what my weird will bids

not how the flesh was meant to be used
not by the spirit subdued and bruised

there's something in the spirit can't be forgiven
icy and soaring past every sun,
earth kicking off from, except like metal,
deliberate, constructed, spun,
slender, suspended, far from home,
iron-glinted, elegant, erect,
dancing away from the body
for the big romance
with intellect

THE LADIES

tous jours is the ladies
and all nights
                    dominable
pasture of the evil hound
  reneguing
bitter source
walled beyond draining

goodbye when I go in
broken daylight
when I struggle on
like normal

a hook to be hung on
a scarlet grave
a thread from the beast
   to the virgin
is me
am my past
what worse admit?

mother-dogged and father-vacant
   she-howling
   and he-wasted
what they call murder in the papers
it didn't happen
but when has that actually mattered?

i have myself to scandalise
my taut and knot of sex
and always the ladies
   and their 'maginations

from rut of cripples
   i try to walk
with the scupperers in me, the bombardiers
pulling the plug on intention
and lining my loving with steel

DIGGING

fallen in a heap
again
why do i keep
falling in a heap?

i got plaster
i got bricks
i got a boxful
of tradesman's tricks
i got cement
well it's still in the bag
there isn't a tap here
that's the drag
i got sand
i got trowels
i got my dad's
good set of rules
  the architect's plan
said build a square
but i read it wrong
and built it in air
he laughed like a demon
when he saw what i'd done
said Won't last a minute
in a good-going sun
dig down there
with the help of your brutes
it won't be a square
unless it has roots
  so i dug
and i'm digging

and i'll dig
but digging's not the trouble
it's getting rid
of the rubble
he specifically said
I don't care what's done
with what you throw out of here
but we're delving to go up again
and the surface must be clear
   and here i'm surrounded
i'm mountained and mounded
with more rubbish than hole
and no barrows at all

fallen in a heap
again
why do i keep
falling in a heap?

THE PRODDY HEEBIE JEEBIES

the proddy heebie jeebies
are bitin' intae me
my voluntary rescue team
has foundered in the sea

the polis stand by helpless
they're feared tae dae a thing
in their constitution
rex is still the king

i lash about quite manful
it doesnae do nae good
a hernia a rupture
i cant digest my food

the boys is whizzing over
land and sea to help
nietzsche blake and a chinaman
they gie the prots a skelp

the proddies come back fightin
frae a base inside my skull
cunnin old buggers o fishers o men
they've drained life to the full

and there i'll have to leave you
this interim report
of rank disturbance of the peace
and take myself to court

THE TRIBE

the tribe is dancing
the tribe is always dancing
because in dancing
there is no peace

peace they won't have
because darkness is
constructed like a
maze they won't go into

the maze makes them dance
round no centre
in no shape
but against and
at their shadows

above them only moon
distant light

they have danced for a thousand years
neversliding
down the past that sleep is
dancing is their drug
in the face of absence
and makes their sleep
another shift

their dance is against the earth
          and that is no dance
their dance is against the sun
          the drought of their birth

and against the monsters who pester their heads
red-beak black-winged birds whose food
is the marrow of the dry dancing stick
man
          and that is no dance

THE DEVIL

Concerning the struggle between man and god
there is only one go-between and he is odd.

He's not in the index of the great ready reckoner
so he fucks up the figures as cipher and sickener.

A hundred Oxford mathematicians using the best
                                                            computers
failed to add up two and two and fell among the
                                                            neuters.

The only living survivor then claimed he had
                                                            discovered
that numbers were the toes of God and should never
                                                            have been uncovered.

Others wouldn't accept as a fault that their numerous
                                                            equations
Didn't reveal why butter and eggs don't satisfy the
                                                            nations.

And many who'd given up good careers for a
parliamentary seat
said: 'If this is what duty and service are like then
power must be a treat.'

Oho at the bottom of all goings on is a big dark
bottomless pull
Which blows its nose up its sleeve and hums:
'I call, I kill, I cool'.

CITY MAN

the soaring inequity
the tumble down might
the striding dwarf
the city man
the plague dweller
the endemic rat
home to illness
and away to fuck
the lamplit scarperer
the denizen of brick
a hundred pleasures at his twiddle tips
and the memory of one sunny holiday up his nose

are we bleeding millions
white to dying with riding our handbags
a race?
more like a bloody rush

more like a kid's sweetie bag
of manufactured muck
burst on the ground
and we
sneaky ratbags
of tenement and terminal
what memories we cherish
what fond tales we'll pass on
of struggles in the sun and wind
and possibly drizzle in the late afternoon

THREE LITTLE GREEN QUARTERS

There's leafs and pools inside to hide in
skins and pods and shells to slide in
there's barks and musk and sands to touch
lots of things in us not human very much
if we want
but we don't but only a few do
for the rest the past is mumbo hoodoo
something sucked and scaled
been transcended
a gold rush trail that's been hauled and ended

i and my self would like to sink into the non
human to the eyes
pleasure of vision the only prize
but know very well the other guys
won't give up their lust
to organise

dissect dead flies
and get ten men working on an other man's whys
they're all at it and out
up and on
eager to get the whole universe mapped
not sensing the pulse of their guts is gone
just as if the spinal cord had snapped
they've not felt yet they're spinning free in space
running in no race
just black
sheep shot out from home in disgrace
to make good or get lost in a distant place
to be forgotten in any case
but the signs that our minds roam on untied lines
are there in what we're waiting for
a martian year one
in our nineteen eighty four
a meeting with strange captains from a master
civilization
who will bend gently over us through galactic curves
and offer what they've learned in an older universe
to help us through our long division
the conquerors of matter
and the absurds of evolution

meanwhile we discover in earth's skies at night
the unidentified flying object guilt
the beautiful round shining space ship god
the dark fast dangerous cigar shape the devil
and the appearance and eclipse in a flash of red
of three little green quarters of our personality
near an ancient burial ground just inside our head.

*

the tower is hanging
the horn's dismantled
the knights are working
in the service industries
and i lie curled in a dirty web
waiting for a horror to inject
the body of what's coming
with the filth its past is made of

THE ENEMIES

the loyal agents of death
the general and the tight-lipped woman
remind us
to rip off our buttons
from our bellies to our throats
and dance

when death has become icy instead of hot
good men have got
to turn from the light
and use
        the drums
        the dance
        the night
to worm up the devils into the day
        and say
Ladies and gentlemen
        on our left
        and on our right
we have both the opponents at bay

and now that we've dumped the humps off our backs
        we may
        see a fair fight
and watch: for the winner won't be either of these
        but an alloy
they'll hammer out of each other tonight

TONITE

tremble, trust not, creep low,
too late!
I am now many,
I walk carrying,
do not bring forth–
what me bastards dragons–
ho no–
I am a quiet lad
known for repose and tempered wrath.
rarely will I go to the theatre
where they play all fancies out,
and pipe my steam en masse.
I have my own most internal
dramatics, most theatrical
innards
where nightly to the tune
of ave a neurosis
persons pass and exchange
greedy tot-bites of information,
slander filth and hear hear o-ism
why part with a dollar to see it done

with frescoes verve and intervals?
oedipus hamlet all that crowd
of murdering i-ambic ma-lingerers
occupy my brain-pot, that cell, that court,
seat and site of the closeted family.
what! most certainly blood doth
not flood me through but printer's ink
and these my talons are only quills.
histories I read merely
to check the facts, corroborate
and set the bounds to my brimming talent
for spectacles and scenes, acts and hacks.
  of course, kings have burned down cities,
carted off booty, on rafts, through blood,
and good men have been hung, by the teeth, the nails,
                                                            the hands, the head,
from the crosses of order, permanence and greed.
  aren't you always at it? I am.
cops and nazis geysering through
my icy glass of contemplation,
skating and cutting me into ruts,
before the furrowed surface fading
feeds them back to the seethy waters.
every day I ice 'em over, deliberate:
why not? I'm due three meals a day
like anyone else. I don't feel called
to sport uniquity yet, though when it stirs
its drug is strong.
                              But those other toiling palaces
of entertainment, archives of secret pacts, called men,
disappoint me terrible. so rarely they give me
a cry or dance from the script I know
they're programmed. just a bit of sound track
                                                                        sometimes

as you pass, or half an overture when a lad
leans forward: 'I don't know if you ever. . .' and stops–
imagining himself the only one contains
the beast and bastardy that comes along
with the nine pound brain and opposable thumb
of man. so long in darkness with his own mad kings,
killing mums, sweet maidens et by monsters
and naked formales bending just his way,
he's not seized yet the one embracing fact:
we are the lads the very men
who humped our mums by massy walls
and put our pa's down in an act of congress,
none but us the ghosts and gods, good and baddies,
who wrought and rended empires the sand still seals
. . . nervously the lad rings off his speech,
smiles sad and says: 'Another time, maybe. No words
for me to tell what I go through.'

Brother! sad man, victim, tomb, ark
of all! how could one word of reported truth
fail to dent me, nick and needle exactly
into the furrows and pockets, quarters and grooves
that make my brain yours, your's caesar's and caesar's
the same as that ignorant dull barman feeds us pints.
Audience, accomplices, witnesses, fellow
fallen, twin birthers, scattered family marked forever
by the contents of our heads, I leave you
to take a bath and comb my hair
in preparation
for
TONITE!

HERO TREK

you don't kill dragons on land no
you don't kill dragons on land
you walk on
            on your back
            your boat
the only dry thing in the mud world
the dragon makes
            sump clog   sump clog
as you walk
to the bit where mist meets fog
and the shitty water whispers
boatford dryness feed us tomcat
sucks your boat
from shoulders to surface
and as you push off the octopus sludge
takes your right foot
            stumpy
for two things–
to let you know what a winner is
and draw the fretty fish
towards your blood

THE CITY

the silver grids of electricity
the nets of rayon
the bulk of iron

man the bow
and boy the arrow
woman the well
and girl the furrow
can't tell now
necessities from ornaments
    tools
    from toys
    masks
    from faces
    crutches
    from crushers

earth water
fire air
        give what we need
food and light
bath and bed
where?

far out of the city
                where the army manoeuvres
far out of the city
                where the hills eat shoes

only one city
        and it's guarded
only one guard
        and it's self
only one self
        it's divided

murder gives birth and adds up the sum
the deaths of three and four make one
the city is guarded
but the king in his palace will still
be murdered

to let these things happen

take my strength from me
take my mind

take my wit from me
take my tongue

take my lies from me
take my mirror

make me low
        down
        flat
        clear

make me bend
        give
        faint
        flow

make me a building
  with no people
let me be empty

make me a hand
  with no fingers

let me be useless

make me a clock
  with no face
let me live now

PRAISES

Let us praise the condition of the onion:
The onion does not drive the motor car
The onion does not go to the place of work
The onion does not enter into union with
unpredictable creatures

But the onion can be destroyed – by disease or damp.
Let us then praise disease and damp
And, since they are separate things,
Let us praise them separately.
  Let us praise damp first:
Damp can destroy almost anything
Damp is great
But damp can be kept out
And damp can be destroyed – by fire or heat.
Let us, for the sake of argument, call fire and heat the
same thing

And let us praise them – it, and damp-proof walls:
Damp-proof walls are great
But they can be destroyed – by fire.
Let us therefore praise fire twice:

Fire is great great
But fire can be kept out
And fire can be destroyed – by damp.
Let us therefore praise damp again, it and fire-proof
walls:

They are great.
But let us now rather praise disease
Which was to be praised after damp in the first place:
Disease can destroy any living thing
Disease is great
But it cannot destroy any dead thing.
Let us therefore praise all dead things:
They do not drive the motor car
They do not go to the place of work
They do not enter into union with unpredictable
creatures

But, also, they do not grow in the dark ground
They do not suit themselves in golden skins
And they do not make us cry when we come into
them.
Let us therefore, finally, praise the condition of the
onion.

THE NEWTON MAN

an irritable man   a grumpy humphie
squared by reason   ringed by fact
shock-proof   disaster-ridden

crank-turning   inch devouring
tickle tensing   tally hoing
vital no   statistics yes

who organises the discovery of matter?
microscopic caligulas   devilish exmechanics
accumulators and cross reference men
lonely plagiarisers in guggenheim monasteries
icecold schizoids in the dungeons of gridgraph

lady godiva had moles on her molecules
and peeping tom won the nobel prize for minute
observation

ALL ALONG THE TORTURED KNIGHTS

All along the tortured knights
the precise demand
to be fitting and upright
to con knowledge
into fruit

we are lumbered and back-logged
with weight and pitch and volume
of past:
repositories not men

not walk about natural;
walk in history, trundled
like trolleyfulls of books

self-taught but not
    -conquered
loaded and so unfree

born into cross and death of kings
battles tomes and revolutions

the simplest man
    is food of his time
its historical jaws
    eat him and shit

the complex broken half-man
(he refers to the author)
turns against his digestion
to let his future be
but often would surrender
for the peace of being swallowed

the next is to break through
the one and only point in time it can –
mine self
which is like being holed
by an anchor
seeks deep bed in my flesh.

time lives in my body
as a full fire
and i, in my small way,
    damp it
till i have the unearthly goodness
    to dissolve

AINT GONNA BE

the island of love   a nest of insects
a coloured wheel   a floating rash
a broken hand   a filthy wish
a timebuilt awkward   a fragment rumour
a frothing nark   a will-less push

underneath
                    you can tell what there was
colleges ago
our mind is the boomerang prince
homes on our heads
and our gravity stretches our necks
we first fell off some thousand years
and keep in touch by eagly watching
it's not a question of going back
it's a foregone conclusion of ploughing through stone
stone is our city
we are our dead

lather our masks in the mirror
and climb into the same rigor every morning
the dead keep regular hours untouched by rain
and button their clothes against swelling
our games are based on the skeletal lurch

and our love
is the irritated mating of sea-things
in dry tanks
our kids are uncodeable
their ciphers fade after a year and a half
our schools are surrounded by lawns not grass

so it goes on
some things were never meant to be, jimmy
and we were one of them
the wet's going away from us all the time
and we sit dotted like currants on a dust heap of flour

aint gonna be none of that gentlefolk cake now
aint nobody left's got them malleable hands

THE WORSTEST BEAST

the worstest beast that swims in the sea
is man with his bathing trunks down to his knee

the worstest beast that goes through the air
is man with his comb to tidy his hair

the worstest beast that bores through soil
is man with his uses for metal and oil

the worstest beast that hunts for meat
is man who kills and does not eat

the worstest beast that suckles its young
is man who's scared of nipples and dung

the worstest beast that copulates
is man who's mixed his loves and hates

the worstest beast that has warm skin
is man who stones himself with sin

he's the worstest beast because he's won
it's a master race and it's almost run

FALLING

falling asleep in an armchair
lets the wind the words
rise
labourers and dons despise
the odd the weird
use fuck the pope and formulas
to keep back feared
walk in light
that's dry and tight
and wonder why the million facts
of sound and sight
won't unite
for all their thousands of boxes of tricks
that add up the info
and answer: nix
and get cheesed off
because politics
always seems to end
in opposites

and all the time a baby cries
saying feed me fill me
I'll devise

I'm warm and wet
I'm form and light
but not the light that hits the skies
I shine in dark
I shake surprise
I feed on snakes
and advertise
through dreams and art and all that's mad and terrifies
I'm here I fill
but you fear you kill
for God's sake reverse
and sprinkle me spray
I shrink I shrivel every day
self-waste and wars are my screams and cries
that your minds torch out of me
your incinerating eyes

LABOUR

the black makes the black black
the black makes the black black
the black makes the black black

the world grows round in orange whorls

its smithereens are held together
by toil by care
sweat of the ox
makes the glue
for casing robots

inside not delicate machinery
inside not warm wet
inside
one spring one clock one bomb

the symbol of labour is a fist
yes
the symbol of labour is a punch
yes
the symbol of labour is a hard knot
a thwart
a dam
a detonation

and the labouring man is black
at heart

END

why should i fear madness?
i'm not in despair
i'm in upsurge
a kind of built-in upsurge
with barriers and antidotes complete

no other problem than to hate me
destroy disrespect condemn me
        up root
        down pour
        blame

i beseech death   i search fire
i look for a sword
to spill my yesterday guts
my careful hoard of self
the only honest thing i do is wank
it's true to the rot
i'm built on ·

i'm built on rot
and shiftiness

i'm keen for the roof to go
and my dead globey eyes

i am an invented man
i am a domestic unit
i am shit
i am digested
i am not a green leaf
i am not a goat
i am nobody's good bite
i am a bullet
and a shattered barrel
i am manufactured
i did not spring
i am not lost

i am bent with sign-posts
i am a mirror fan
i am plagued by creeps
by the worried furrowed lines
of knitting myself together
which makes me sick

but a little dry sick
not a bloody coloured eruption

the care i take to carry on

i am not a disease
i am a crust of health
a little round rabbit turd
that's learned to roll
i am the unnatural daffodil
that wouldn't die at the end of its week
i am a dry stick
pretending to be an insect
i invent my day
every day
and i am a sandy well
i am as fertile
as the board tongue of a burning crab
and i am surrounded by barbed wit

collect the ash-can while you may
but i regret throwing anything away
you never know
when an old sock, say,
might come in handy
to stuff an impulse a baby's cry
a slender shoot of some sort

i would ask the aerial god
to bombard me
if he was

i would ask the earth

to devour me
if she were
but i know
that one must kill one
be self-undone
and stand like in dreams
over one's body with a gun
saying
where gone?
what now?
glee (?) glee (?)

NICE

nice to be on a pasture nibbling
                    bell
    and a call at sundown

humpled in steam through the night
slosh o' mornings
and found for snoring winter
not built that way though me
ici always uneasy

    'cos i always icy
not like the flock the likeable lump me
for i would die down if i did lie down
in an animal warmth
their sleepy envelope of one complaisant skin

THE PATIENT

My drought-grown frown of knowledge –
What a way to die!
Having one's convictions kicked by passers-by.
That goes, and we go down –
Slowly, oh slowly. (Certainly this is not time)

Down, and the grin disappears, that was the last
Of consciousness – no laughing – the dark the real
dark
With the last light a shadowed disc.

See me now with only a memory of clarity:
Hospitalised – for there will be many
Nurses and doctors to deal with this case.

'This patient has many of the symptoms of advanced extension of the ego and intensification of the metabolism (due to immersion in uncovered time stream).'

Humour: a puppy in the dark.
Talent: moderate to extortionate.
Constitution: tarred.

I'd say to get nowhere in thirty years (called fourteen of real endeavour) is not bad going. Considering all those who think they have arrived at the age of 25 and build upon it without a second's hesitation. Good.

I know where I stand. I stand where the manhole cover was. That is me you see descending gracefull, elbows ajut. I will leave my hat upon the pavement (brim too wide) and whoever it fits can claim my case-notes.

Me simple, now thirty, made to start,
Not clean but clear, not head but heart,
Not clean heart but clear head to begin
With Al
No other
Let noise decrease
Which is to do with money.
Cash, I guess, will be found
As before.

I'll rest – not from the task (spelt huge)

But from the hullabaloo and hum of intellect.
That's the noise that even the dopiest are tuned to:
Its elements ego cash mass and time
Cash: the abstract survival
Time: the expenditure of self in pursuit
And mass: the number in competition which speeds
time up.
And so we go out – to work
Let them – only wars ever stop them, for a while
Not let them win, though – too grim
(This is my world too)

Well, then, I will toddle on purposeful
(yea, me!)
not possessed of etc
knowing nothing
And so, being a thousand doors,
I will see the fault in the heart
Because I have unlearned.

At thirty I will add up my sums:

Love, possibly
Sex, frequently
Vileness, radical.

HELLO, HALO MOON

when was simplicity?
when the moon glowed blue?
not from a hundred feet down
to a hundred miles up
is one shard or bubble
of good grub
but we are speaking arrows
shaved shaped sharpened
and shot

where we land is not to choose

I think it was something in the mud
got high on oxygen
and went subtle beyond decency
what am I but shiny mudster?
accomplished turdling?

a roman a jew and a greek
a german man and others
they're all beneath and shafting through
this specialisation of god-verboten lusts

so I would be clever to be happy?

I would be a monster of simple intelligence
such as never in . . .
takes genius now to bite an apple true –

to fuck sweat fight and fill
        in all modes latent –
we're past all that.
        call it a shadow across us if you wish
but it had shrapnel in't
        and clings like birth
and this is not even to mention a tail
        man is manx but monkey still
what a laugh we are!
        somehow it is always evening with us
downtrodden day all time
        no softly nightwards slowly snuggling
night is bath
        and we've no slack or 'linquish in us
to lavish or soak in suds
        only triggered flight
'hello, halo moon
        we've bitten through
and fearsome's truth:
        there is no doubt
a most terrible thing has been done –
        landing on your powdered plains
we planted a flag
        a flag!
half a million years of bones demanded it
        possession is our peace
there's no rest in us, no rooting mode,
        we sign things and go on
the ant is mute and orderly

men are whithering and crossed
and how dangerous our quiet ones are
take me away from the crowds of respectables
their effluent's acid
their votes are rusted tetanus swords
and the women of them are thin-strung biters
all the laziness in the world won't suffice
this is a saga
and everyone's signed
endless lotions of honey poured
from bosomed and beautiful-
buttocked barrels
couldn't stick or stem us
from stampede.
the pleasantest little dad in his beanrow
of a sunday morning
is hammering like a hornet in hell through history
and the harder he stands
the faster he gets.

*

The Holy Ghost came to me
in the shape of a lamb's tail
and I said No

The Holy Ghost came to me
in the shape of a candle
and I said No

The Holy Ghost came to me
    in the shape of a pen
and I said No

The Holy Ghost came to me
    in the shape of a black pig
and made a mess all over my living-room
    and I said Yes, oh Jesus, yes.

transcend me, forgive me, shatter me, mark me

TICKY BOT

Ticky Bot
Ticky Bot
What do you say!

  going a big journey
  no have to pay

Ticky Bot
Ticky Bot
How can that be?

  go is by moonlight
  shady and free

Ticky Bot
Ticky Bot

Share us your boon

gladly but can't sir,
your air is noon

CHRONOS

A man wi' a great big beard
A met;
Said: 'Don't be feared
If ye get wet.

Run twenty years
On nature's liquor,
Hit velocity
An die the quicker.

Let the watter rin
Ower the top o yer heid,
And don't come up
Till they think ye're deid.

When the crowds are away
An the stars are out,
Land back on earth
Wi a helluva clout.

Then dance a dozen
Steps or two
On yer empty grave:
Ye'll do, ye'll do.'

NOTICE

in the outposts of the dark
the long weed the tattered frags
in the tumble down stand still wreck
of tolerance and easy going
I
am muted
a ring lost from a dead queen
      I am parted from the other
because I'm playing
been very human
for too long
dandled everybody
it's not been my way to be bitter and savage in a pub
but from now on
I AM NOT IN

what a hateful arrogant man
not to be in

but that's the notice I'm giving

RENEGADE MECHANEGO

i have not rendered mercy
      i am taken apart
i have not been obedient
      and so i am forced
i have not been silent
      i will have to be told

i am looking for a lord
i am looking for a lord
i am looking for a lord
i have read the books and discoursed on roots
i have loved ideas and nodded my head
i have suggested diets and fed on cobbles
oh i have diagnosed 'um
        been self a pest
well i am guilty and that is reaction
        by the liberal light
well i am humble and there's treason
        to the liberal light
well i need, i bleed, and that's heresy
        to the upstander intellect
been using reason to undo reason
and have hung on to reason;
and that's madness and
to hell with the light
ten years bent to the block,
and not dropped the blade
        not broke the head
        not bathed the block
 – madness
for what is it but death that contains me?
my hidey hole house
my regulation habits
my frightened lusts?
yea, i have been cleverer than the cleverest
and not believed what i said myself.
so am i stiff stuff, cool kill,
i am resister intellect, renegade mechanego,
        and i still will
            will still.

THE EMPEROR'S DESPATCH

come to me tonight
on flowering feet
this meeting drags
and I don't care
about their troubles on the bloody border
two furry tribes have taken a stone town
and my generals are mad
to go and slay
but my mind is closing from them while they talk
I almost feel I can feel your legs
and see your witty tits

I remember the first time I saw you dancing
and thought: That I fancy
easy for an emperor except
too easy and never knows
what he wins his women with
gold and the left-hand seat
or what

so I never made the usual summons
for you to come and know
what was expected
for rumour to reach fact
and you be famous
for a few nights' work:
how long will this thing last,
the little bitch
with tiny breasts
and northern hair?
long enough to make her worth a visit?

or shall we wait
till he wakes tired?
again

but I kept your father here
in search of business
and found out ways to meet you as you passed
by the river or in the garden walks
to let you see I lingered on your looking
and was waiting for your shyness
                              or your smile
untill we talked
as if I was not the key to towers and kingdoms
and you were not being honoured by a glance

and now that we've both known each other naked
and I have thrown a vase just missed your head
and you have run away all grim and pouting
and I didn't send to get you from your aunt's
  I know my cloak's just cloth that hangs on shoulders
that my crown is just a hat that makes me great
that you are half my empire and my equal
and that soldiers kill and conquer on tired feet

so anyway I'm sending you this letter
(they think I'm making notes on their campaign)
        come tonight
        for sunset walk in garden
        wear your blue and yellow
        and stay mine

THE MEN

the trumpeting warriors
take their weapons apart
and grin at the gristle and skin
        that's in

end of the kids in and out of their feet
end of the women at the doors in the street

churches and towers now free to be clean
in their carriage of fire from the sky to the earth
free to be built without depth but with height
to celebrate air in column and beam
        no more stooping and sweat
        looseness and wet
but back to a deadly band again
of black hard pure helmeted men

THE SWINE

The swine hangs on,
The swine hangs on to power,
The townsfolk mutter round the tower:

'Roast him, toast him,
Thin his blood.
Try fire first,
Then try flood.

Char the timbers,
Crack the stone.
Make him marrow
In a splintered bone.

Then he'll tumble,
Our hot meat.
Then we hack him.
Then we eat.'

WEST MAN

between gold and iron still hammered,
each living one of us,
keen to jingle and cleave,
in the west, that is, that I know of,
where the wind is red.

bearded in boats, they cut the ocean:
we singe air. The word's still: 'On'
which means To The End.

we cut the balls of god and killed his woman,
we'll take our freedom at all expense,
our eyes are screwed to telescopes,
our wind blows us off into space,
blows from a mouth
too wide to smile,
too deep for disobedience.

west man, maybe man, but I only say what I know,
is a killer, has hurt himself worst as must be,
and he stands now on the roof of the planet,
bare and pricked,
on an unleaved branch of a last tree,
listening to nothing,
                                        but the sound of himself,
thinking.

HERO TREK (2)

to stand by the edge of an earthquake
  see the bonny buildings go
  and walk away saying Aye
  but not me

to see the power and resist the power
  creeping along the boundaries
  one foot
  in and
  one foot
  out
eaten up to the knees the one time
kicking back fish-puss the next
crying aloud at the balancing of it
laughing because bubbled monster's breath
is a joke to the wanderer's mind
that hasn't caught what the game is yet –
eat or be et –
the rule where mud meets dry with wet

the sun's there – oh
but red and low
'n' no stars show
to lonelies limping

for this is where
from right or left
broken land
or cooking sea
some how some things some ones can
take a witless man
and turn him inside out
for no other end
than to see
what he has
in the way
of abundance

TODAY

they were arguing over the dead lady's body
the surgeon said
freeze her. give me ten years
and unlimited money
for certain machines
she will walk, breathe
the man from the funeral parlour said
that is obscene
with my hands i will give her beauty and peace
more than is fair

she will stay loved in the dreams
of us trapped in air
when i hurried into the bed and said
bells confetti priest cake
i'm marrying future and past now
and this is the one i take

JOURNEY

Who is my friend?
He who rides with me.
Who rides with me?
None but my horse

Have I no friends then?
Yes I have many.
They each ride alone
With none but their horse.

Who is my lady?
My lady's my honour.
What's flesh and blood?
The vessel of love.

Who am I then?
I am the rider:
From darkness to light
One two three and four.

And what is the forest?

The forest is knowing.
We ride through knowing
Till we reach All-Now.

And what is the meaning?
La la tara dido.
And what is the purpose?
La la tara day.

IDIOTS ARE FREELANCE

1963–1970

apple cake distributed
between the poor
not one asking
excuse me,
where
do these apples
grow?

‘TINY NIPPLED MEN’

tiny nippled men wander through the auld toon
in delicate high voices they cry
‘we are what you're coming to’

‘get away fae me, ye daft poofs’
the big drunk labourer shouts
and falls down the steps into the bog in the
grassmarket

*

THE MORAL CODE

if the hair of thy neighbour offend thee
pluck it out

*

HITCH-HAIKU

nae hat
an the cauld rain fallin

dearie me

PERSON

i have no thumb
i am a little
deformed

i don't wear gloves
but i suffer very much
from the insolence
of those who are thumbed
and find in that
their distinction

*

great
tae be hunners o burds
an sit in trees
an wash yer nebs
in rainy leaves

*

TRIBUTE

glasgow's full of artists
they're three feet high
and eat sherbet dabs

*

AND SO IT GOES ON

and the wife is the mother
and the wife is the house
and the wife is the cooking pot
cooking glue

and the husband is the son
he makes a journey every morning
and makes it back every night
not an hour late
not a minute late
not a second late
is best

the mother grub is waiting on the table

*

I made myself a bonnet
from a woman's hair
and walked with her body
and mine
          till it tore

*

KNOX (1)

the old scots grim man
            with the chin
eats an apple on the bus

he hides it in his pocket between bites

            for fear of the animal
            for fear of the people

*

YOUNG POLITICIAN

What a lovely, lovely moon.
And it's in the constituency too.

*

DADDY

Is it true we all used to have hair on our backs?
Yes, son.
And is that why some people used to wear hair
                                        shirts all the time?
No. That was for an opposite reason
   called desperate grovelling trauma.

A SCOTCH POET SPEAKS

Och, I wish you hadn't come right now;
You've put me off my balance.

I was just translating my last wee poem
Into the dear auld Lallans.

*

why do i laugh at the pope?
because the size of his hat
                                        tells me
he is not humble

*

the devil rules,
   we call him reason
the actual light
   we see by

and to sleep
   we take pills
for fear of night
   its invigorating gods

*

the vicar is not an idiot
he is the vicar

idiots are freelance

*

the rival diagnosticians
agree
    to dissect

*

a pity
about the Constituent Assembly

HAWKER

PASSPORTS TO REALITY !
PASSPORTS TO REALITY !
and he actually had
they were clear rounded mouldings of glass
fashioned
to fit the eye

*

at the bottom of the deepest pit
  a baby is fighting a snake
above an engineer phones the owners:
'Nothing left here but the rats Mr Farthing.
Fill her in'.

FIND

while i was out firefighting
i found a dead deer
roasted

lying like Christmas
near a fresh well

it was a find
and good to eat
and all the better
for the accident
of hunger

*

– There were terror, envy and greed in him.
– Yes, but was he reliable?

LINKSY

today it is bubbles
last week it was chain mail
and tomorrow it may be
intricate lacework

ice water and steam

are (not) the same
   though you find fish in all of them
and also in flame

*

The fire is put out that threatened the city.
The watchers walk wistful murmuring: 'Pity'.

*

LOVE AT FIRST

What the heart sees
   is not the other
but a shadow sampling
   of the taste of self

*

– So this is the bathroom?
How beautiful you have made it.

– Yes. It had always been my dream
to capture the freshness of a hospital
in my home.

*

relaxation:
it passes for wisdom
in the Lowlands

*

stoned the god dead
we stoned the god dead
and put together from the bits in our head,
continually,
something called NEW

*

certainly the remedy's
inside the disease
and the meaning of being ill
's to bring the eye
to the heart

*

CONFESSIO

'I put the peas in Galileo's telescope'

*

stony
yes it's stony
aye it's stony
but it's *town*

*

solely to recall you
is my work
sister
sad gamester
fire eaten

*

a rider is dragged to the grave
   and his moon's cut off
   it's not very brave
but what other dark forest do we live in?

*

MEMORY

A little dry leaf
fluttered out of his book.

‘Her name was Griselda.
I loved her. Look.’

*

the story is drowning in the terrible river

*

TARA

tara for now the tadpole said
and tucked his tadtail round his head
i'll sink to the bottom but i won't be dead

*

DEAR AVALANCHE

1973–1974

purificatio
the hands   *the bowl*
the fire   *the water*
mercy

Where's the party? Bring on the mob.
Let's talk about old times, art or god;
Anything than lie here,
Humbled and odd.

*

I have no doubts
about my fitness to love you
I am fit to die

*

We love till we're weak
and watch as the other comes with us
into non-entity

*

And when you crept into the bed,
crying, mumbling:
'Nothing, 'snothing left,
's all going to go,'
I put my arm around you
and was glad

*

must get past
enjoying our enjoyment
let the invisibles feed
without interruption

*

You burble on about 'female conditioning',
And I remember fifteen years in a 'male' hell.
For God's sake, let's discard
This robe of reasons
and take the pain
Without complaint or name.

*

– This, at last, is my father's door
– I see. But why is it standing,
Disconnected,
In the middle of a wasteground,
Shut?

*

lady
    I have loved
sister
and great mother
what fourth are you?
it must be
                child

*

Princess, you are out the well
And not mine
Your own marriage to solitude
Makes you Queen

*

If there were no polarity
  There'd be no hilarity
And God's broken body
  The world we make up

*

all of us clever devils
taking so long
to let intellect go
crystal with a little self
in every eye

*

I came to you in discord
You took me in love
 – death of a fear
And another feather for the wings
Of a young hermaphrodite

*

I'm a fool
 – always afraid of that –
now I know the alternative
is to be a knave

*

I saw my sister
with a tear in her eye
and I was pleased

to see her cry
for I knew she felt
how much she must melt
to feel more to melt more
to be liquid

*

now that the mad bone is quiet
(You know, the one that rattled in the greedy bowl?)
I expect we'll hear other tunes

*

I am your master
my mistress is lost in you
I cannot wait

*

The lighthouse is real
Neither the drunken keeper
Or the wicked wreckers
Alter that.

*

How many you are
  that I love the one of
that pushes me away
  and I don't mind

*

Remember what we struggle with
's not yours or mine
but human
and of this time

We're not sick but living vessels
of dis-stress
that must feel to the utmost
and be broken to be healed

and whatever weapons the powers shall wield
we must yield, and yield, and yield

*

If I cry now it's not from ache
But selfish relief that at last I can love.
What a strange journey it has been
Through the modern obscene.

*

Tears on my cigarette
How can I smoke it, it is so wet?
How can it stay in trembling lips?
And how can I smile through all this?

Because love is leading me through
Love is leading me through

*

I'm an apprentice
and this broken heart's my test-piece
of faith and strength and skill

*

two years I've done nothing
years I've been nothing
I want no thing
I know nothing
now here's a new nothing
a fond nothing
a nothing I like

*

be gentle with yourself as well, my son,
not the first
no reason to be last
in offering acceptance

*

she has turned out for the moment
to be a faithless girl
well, her pain continues

*

You are not alone
I am here, in your heart
If it ever seems you are abandoned, ask me
And I will answer.

Much is up to you;
Your efforts are appreciated
But they are nothing beside the fact
That we are here now.
You are not received according to merit,
You are welcomed as a medium for ourselves.
Your happiness which follows is a side-effect.

Remember for you at the moment,
It is the heart, always the heart.
Don't get too far into solitary pursuits
Or take pride in any achievements:
To love and to suffer for love
Far greater than any spiritual self-discipline.
Don't forget Alison.
Work on her poems and give them to her.
We are waiting in her
As in you:
We will all meet at some point.

*

every time I learn something
it is: to obey

*

now, in the midst of phantoms,
I can still think clear

*

take me
I am for taking
not: tired
not: frightened
just: ready

*

Please, no instant trickery
of LIGHT!

*

dear avalanche, who sent you
– not sure.
why, I guess.

*

mind in two:
Hungry Beast debates
with Broken Voice
subject: nature of bliss
self waits to hear sentence
image of Alison rises
sitting cross-legged
on mat in heart-room

*

at nos 1 and 2
we are learning what we have to learn
mainly, not to want
and how to destroy old knowledge

how's about though
agreeing to enrol each other
in the Academy at no 3
where the guardians are invisible
day and night are the courses
laughter and silence
serve the meals?

*

you sirens in black
I'm broken gold
can't even wave
I've two ears to hold

*

I cannot understand
what is a nunnery?
what is an empire
what is an axe or a rose?
and there are the stars
and what is this pain?
and to whom do I bow my head?

*

it's late and I eat
my emergency pie
but which is most dangerous –
the time, or it, or I?

*

O my love, where is she?
Who am I to serve?
What am I to be?
I will to be a sword.
A sword in no one's name
Can have no victory

I wait and am instructed
I learn from being alone
Yet I am lost without her
Being only one

*

peace, brother, peace;
not alone, not unknown,
windows are open
you will hear the call
and answer with all that you are

*

If there is some mist in the morning,
  Uncreated wanting in the eyes,
Sit in it gently, without fear:
  By light, it disperses and dries

*

Do you see how now we're the dream?

It's not just that things
Are not what they seem.

But that by choice
And act and voice
We become what we are
In the scheme

*

it wasn't you
it wasn't me
who is it at no 3?

*

SUMMMATIO

Were making love
and I reckon
he / she was near to being born
when I / you, was it you / I, said No.
and my body became the sepulchre
of an angel decomposing

so what does the lone man do?
no other than dedicate his life again
: to crystal
: to reception
: to obey

*

nothing's invented, nothing's real
only clue given is how you feel

oh slender tender thread of truth
that spins us out
gets tangled snagged and shudders
at requests for proof
can never be seen by day or night
yet always so softly comes floating back
over traffic and through TV roofs
when thought's abandoned
or the heart is light

*

when you see us stumbling
and when you hear us mumbling
be sure you touch our hands
and say: You too?

THE GUARDIANS ARRIVE

1974–1976

What I must believe:
This tender flesh to radiate,
The web of pain
Turned filigree
By kindness

THE CITY OF MAN

Moon to the left of me,
Sun to the right:
Watch through the window
Arrival of night.

My candle, my kettle,
My pen and my books;
All I give the dark forest
Yet is hard looks.

Still paying debts
To the city of man
That bred me civil
According to plan;

Gave me a cap,
Short socks and a rule,
Sent me hopeful, un-
Knowing to school;

Taught me and beat me,
Scolded and praised me
'Cos I was clever,
Till they had dazed me.

Left at eighteen,
Hole in the heart,
Frightened and sick;
One friend, art.

Rather a desire

Of freedom I'd read
Which matched the dreams
And visions that said:

'Never, no never,
No matter what,
Believe or collab-
Orate in the plot.

Death possesses them,
Rigid I;
Don't stop to quarrel,
Don't wait, fly'.

Oh yes, but I crawled,
Went sideways and stopped
To look at blood
Where knees been lopped.

And I lay and cried,
Thought and dreamed
And understood so much
I screamed.

And slowly through frozen
Strata of pain
I loved one person,
Then loved again;

Gradually healing,
Able to walk:
And what followed that?
Mainly – talk.

Ironic analysis,
Political books,
And always mirrors
To check on looks;

The biting tongue
That passes for wit,
But my dreams were true,
Said : 'Jackson – shit'.

I wrote them down,
Listened, or tried;
Each miserable year
Saw a knot untied.

The misery was sex,
Turned to a demon –
A ruined hunger,
Desperate for women.

But frightened and arrogant;
Fantasy ruled:
All the hot negatives
They'd ruled and schooled.

So I married and, children,
You know what I did:–
Where I couldn't control
I resented and hid.

Although it takes two,
I was the one;
Takes grace to forgive
What I have done.

Lied and revenged,
Bullied and used;
Still frightened and fighting
To get defused.

Was work of death,
Protestant machine;
Industrial product
Made of flesh – obscene.

And though I've altered
To the service of it,
It'll be some time
Before Jackson has quit.

I'm listening to you,
Wind and moon;
I've never moved fast,
I'm coming soon.

There's a date agreed
For this to be through
When I'll be washed clean
And walk simply in blue,

With moon to the left,
Sun to the right;
And, beyond, the great powers
That make day and night.

THIS IS IT

This ground this dream these myths
This time this place this river
We broken people, this ugliness, this empty,
Not yonder, not elsewhere, not the fault of,
None of this caused by causes accessible
To ology, ism or hate;
There's been no mistake here, no wrong turning:
This is the sum of our fate
This is it
This is where we stand and make choice,
See what we've done and accept it as ours ,
Read the world till it comes transparent
And then be ready for Voice,
For loosening the grip of matter from our minds:
Re-assertion of the Infinite
Re-admission of the Divine
This is it
This hysteria this ignorance these cages
These times this violence this darkness:
They're what we believe and feel – written on the world
And when we sicken of looking at shadows
We can look for the light within
There is light but first we find
What throws the shadows
    Bitter reckoning, painful wrestling, guilt
Quite startling, to minds unused to struggle,
Consciences accustomed to blame another.

    Ah then the stories become realities
    Then the myths grow wings and fly

Then the creatures we tidied away
Come back to sting and cackle and cry

Ah then the mind begins to wander
Then the mask begins to crack
Then one tear that slips unasked for
's welcome like mercy to soul on the rack

For see how badly we've treated the earth:
We have denied there was feeling in feeling things
We have denied there was life in living things
We have extinguished and mutilated species
We have analysed the adrenalin of frightened creatures
Wearing blinkers, we have said: 'I can't see it'.
Clad in iron, we have said: 'I can't feel it'.
We have handled butterflies with tongs and said:
'This is nothing but fragments'.

All to be reckoned, all to be paid for
By each living soul
So

If unsure, then good, for therefore attention
If lost, then good, for therefore find
If pain, then good, for therefore openings
If alone, then good, for therefore listen
If hardship, then good, for therefore strength
If poor, then good, for therefore simple
If death, then good, for therefore birth

THE GUARDIANS ARRIVE

the guardians arrive and say tenderly:
'take the little man out of his bunker
been fighting too hard
give him a platter with bread
and a sugar bun
put sups of milk on his table
until he sees
show him soft things
bends in rivers
balls of mud
floating cloud puff
and the end of a long day
reflected on a wall
when he wakes say:
creep don't run
rest don't work
listen don't ask
millions before you and
millions coming
all made room for
washed and welcomed
everything that falls
is falling
out of place
into place
when you go fighting
you push it off
grow small not tall
trying to set and struct into certainty
raises a storm
no escape from

for storm is aimed
it is the rebellion of the soft particles
whose track is formlessness
and to whom knowledge is war
    the spider's blown and lands
    and can man
    but an ounce for armour is a
    ton for failure
    where chance is treated as hostile
    when
    it's only
    always
    your weather'

*

– As the Titanic sank, did you take part in the hymn singing?
– Actually no; I was downstairs in the saloon,
calculating how much whisky it would take
to render such a large block of ice interestin
to a travellin man such as meself.

DOMINIE HOMINIS

You shoulda seen their faces
When A put them through their paces.
'Oh here', they cried, 'the race is
No meant to stand such pain'.
So A tightened up the braces

An tapped their dear wee faces
An said: 'Look, friends, your place is
Most emphatically not to complain.
Ye've lost all ma respect,
Ye've half the planet wrecked,
An yet yer villas are bedecked
Wi yer ill-gotten gain.
So A'm stepping up the agony
An screwin up the screw
Till ye remember on Antigone
An whatsisname the Jew.
For ye're lackin in all dignity
That comes through resistance
An until ye get it right,
If ye'll pardon my insistence
A'm gawntae make ye bleed;
For A'll gladly lend assistance
Tae gie a body distance
An ma engine wi eight pistons
'll come drivin through yer heid.
For ye've got away wi murder
An ye're not gettin any furder
Till A hear ye cryin 'Mercy!'
An admittin tae yer need.

*

Nothin the matter wi me, pal.
Just the people A seem tae attract.

*

– There is love.
– Where?
– Lying by the window weeping.
– Is that love?
– Yes, it is a child
For the moment
Prevented.

ON CONTEMPLATION OF YOUR LOST INFINITE

what the devil do you mean
by closing down
on scope?
I abash you with my heart
I glare you with my tele-vision
I dangle you accusingly
over sinks full of unwashed abysses
I tackle your opportunism at the knees
I fry your battery intellects
I piss on your politics
I beg to remind you of the hundred million empty
bowls
every night every morning: empty bowls
stuff yourself with goodies, you sickening remnants
I loathe your Christmas
the tinkle of tills is not like bells to me, brother,
and the £7.50 box of DRESS YOUR KIDDIE AS A
METAL MONSTER AS SEEN ON TV

is not exactly a gift
yes I stand amazed as you turn your children
deliberately
into greedy paws
demanding little channel flickers whose proudest cry is:
Don't have to, if I don't want to.
Floggin? No, no I am not one of that party, sir.
I do not intend to interrupt the well-deserved downfall
of this diabolic cacophony by any unceremonious
act of violence

*

It's changing every day, moving very fast,
just managed, in fact, to cast my slowness
like a cloud round the heads of the horses
as I slowly shifted up out of the interior
into the coachman's seat, and
took the reins!
Horses still not very sure about this
but, by God, I am
I'll let them run as fast as they want –
up hill.

*

OFF

I accept the quest
My weapon is ready
Please tell me again though
Before I go
Which is the dragon
And
Which the princess?

*

'No, no,' she said,
'You shall not have a kiss'.
'Right! that's it', I thought,
Head for the abyss.

ALONE IN A ROOM

I don't know if I can speak to you unless
Unless
Unless you have been bitten by the dream.
Have you?
Been bitten by the dream?
Have you begun to get the idea that this
That this
That this is one of many possible worlds?
But the one that you're in at the moment that you're
in it
Really is,
And that you better believe that, sort of friend,
Because it's your life they're after?
Yes, the deep true dream that lives in front of you,
Have you been touched by its alternate fingers?
Oh so cold and oh so warm.
'Does this thing come to do me good or do me harm?'
And, do you know, these questions do not
matter, chum.
Warm or cold, good or bad, it's come, your time has
come –
To die.

No, I don't know if I can speak to you unless
Unless –
Have you ended in a room, have you, ended,
in a room?
I mean alone in a room
Without a chance of leaving it until
Until you have exhausted – something –
Like the load of lies you've been carrying for years
And maybe found that one way is to weep it out in
tears.

Yes, have you ended in a room unable to decide
To stand or lie or eat or fast or go or come?
Begun to get the feeling you don't exist
That everything you believe in especially your
cleverness
Is an utterly rigid deathly construction made of mist
Put together every morning by the energy of fear
i.e. of hell
Which builds conglomerates frontiers armies and
your putrid little self as well?
Oh I don't know if I can speak to you,
Frankly, baby, I don't know if I can like you very
much
Unless
You have admitted that you are a great big squashy
Ungainly frightened puking bawling crawling lying
mess.
There's only one thing to believe and I don't have to
be told it
So if you're beginning to come up with some interesting points about all this, then can it, look you, hold it.

I don't think I can speak to you, you see,
Unless you've spent a long time thinking about the pain
And particularly, is it in every thing or body
Or just me, me, me.

Have you?
Well, this is the relief I bring to you: it is we.
Please believe me it is we, please believe me it is we.
You hardly exist, your pain's the world's
And that's the clue that you can follow till you're free.

THE KILLER QUEEN AND THE INFANT PROJ

The killer queen and the infant proj
Ah! they are the two that figure here
Not alone
Oh not alone
That would be most unfair strife
No, there's a husband and a wife
Upstairs in the headbox
And the rows! the bad meals!
The narky feeling in the guts
From the love they haven't made.
All? No, not all:
For always, through, fighting through,
That one thin blade, that one green shoot,
That elemental wire that seeks to connect.
Oh the blossom building, the bulb waiting

To light, to flower through, to find its way up
through:
Heaviness, opposition, downright stupidity,
faulty fuses,
Parched ground, paving stones, cries of the poor,
whips of the owners, noise of business,
Always *through*, calling, worming, seeking:
Oh its gratitude for one drop rain, one kind word,
The welcoming woman, the solid friend, the wink in
the dark,
The scrambled eggs, the 'You can lie down here, man'.

Yes this century, smell the burnings, taste the lies in
the ties,
The attitudes which are *de rigeur*.
Scented death, who didn't eat it? Who wasn't fed it?
Called discipline-absence, guilt-obedience,
character-fear.
And always *through*, seeking its way, to light to air
to earth to water
– the shoot, the blade, the flaming wire.
Stood on mud and praised the Lord
Stood in shit and loved the stars
Stood on concrete blessing clouds
Stood on carpets cursing tellie
Lay on pillows cursing she
And always *through*, the voices calling, the child
is crawling,
The Infant Proj:–
Wading, evading, harking the wind, sifting the
messages,
Winnowing the crap;
Striking upwards, stretching limbs, rearing spinal,
learning holds;

Gratitude always, reaching teachers, finding kindness,
Falling down, cursing and nursing, laughing and crying
At rubbishy self;
Onward though,
Growing stronger, staying awake longer, the Infant Proj.
Killer Queen less a foe now, more a burden,
As she dies, falling on top of him,
Dirtily dying, putrefying in his body, as he crawls;
Keeps on going, sometimes singing, sometimes muttering,
Hurrah Hurrah the Infant Proj, phagocytes busy,
Fiery fever overheating, fantasy flowing, gaskets blowing,
Can't stop now, must keep going,
Death in his cells
Which he turns
To life.

TELL

the arrow's in the apple
the boy is live
while the father trembles
at the arrogance
of his integrity

DEAD MAN'S CREEK

Oh I hid my head from the mighty wind,
Yes I hid my head from the mighty wind.
But the wind didn't mind, no, it came right in;
No, the wind didn't mind, it came right in.

And I ran away up Dead Man's Creek,
Yes, I ran away up Dead Man's Creek,
And what did I hear, but a dead man speak?
Yes, that's what I heard, I heard a dead man speak.

And this is what he said, said Welcome, friend;
Yes, that's what he said, said Welcome, friend.
You can stop off runnin' 'cause you've reached the end,
You can stop off runnin' 'cause you've reached the end.

But I didn't believe him, and I jumped for shelter,
No, I didn't believe him, and I jumped for shelter.
And the place I jumped to, was a helter-skelter,
Yes, the place I jumped to, was a helter-skelter.

Round and down and round and down
Down and down and around and round
Till I hit with a thud in the mud on the ground,
Yes, I hit with a thud in the mud on the ground.

And here I'm resting with a hundred more,
The lame and the weary and the sick and the sore.
Yes, here I'm resting with a hundred more,
The lame and the weary and the sick and the sore.

We don't do much, but we don't tell lies;
No, we don't do much, but we don't tell lies.
When you go underground you lose the lids off
your eyes,
Yes, when you go underground you lose the lids off
your eyes.

So, welcome, welcome, welcome, friend.
Yes, welcome, welcome, welcome, friend.
Have no fear, we all meet here in the end,
Deep in the ground where you grow and mend.
Down with the dead men, you're welcome, friend;
So don't be afraid: we're going to meet, going to meet
going to meet in the End.

AM I EITHER

Am I either?
I am neither.
I am neither
This nor that.

Do you claim me?
You can't same me.
I am neither
Round nor flat.

Are you singing?
Then I'm listening.
Are you looking?
I'll look too.

You forgetting?
I'll remember.
You for going?
I'll help you through.

Want a burden?
Upsadaisy!
Need a rest?
Tut tut tut.

Want a fight?
I'll stand behind you.
Want a kiss?
I'll stand in front.

I'm kind of going
Kind of staying
Kind of no-ing
Kind of yea-ing.

More exactly
What I'm saying:
I am neither
This nor that.

*

They threw me a bone.
  I cried: Where's the meat?
They said: It's to bite on,
  Not to eat.

I PRAY

I pray
I pray first of all for us all
    for the warm walking zone of humans round the
                                                world
    the voice heart mind toes and fingers of the earth
    guardians gardeners caretakers victims refugees

I pray for us here, walled doored hedged in the cities
    and their pathetic curtained rooms
    maddened starved and frozen by our own
                                                mechanics
    by the stone we have so gracelessly cut,
    constructed and entombed ourselves in

I pray for our hearts that we should hear
    and that we should become what we are
                                                becoming,
    brothers and sisters

I pray that we have courage to fight death
    especially in ourselves our lovers and friends
    whatever the cost whatever the pain and that we
                                                understand
    this seeming cruelty is in the service of love

I pray that we have the strength to stand alone when
                                                we need to
    and find again how to attend to the energies of
                                                earth and star

I pray that we discover how to be small falling and
                                                weak

how to be gentle to the wounds in others
how to give and receive balm from each other

I pray that we learn that friendship food and love
are not simply pleasures but communion
and that duty, debt, service and work
are not separate from them

I pray that we won't let death-in-life conquer us
as it has conquered many faces many states many
times
I pray because blow by blow by blow I have been
shown
I must pray this prayer every day

SO MAYBE WHAT I'M SAYING IS

Thanks you for your invitation to the Hermitage
which you so purely expressed the meaning of.
I was tempted –
to die, to end one's affairs,
to enter with others on the true search,
to be subject to discipline,
to powerful reflectors,
to where love is a sword,
where counter-agents to the self-deluding mind
(you can't make it on your own)
would tell the truth and make ever harder demands.
I was tempted
but whether or not it is my weakness

whether because it is I'm not ready,
I'm not coming.
No, I can't live without a woman
(though, in fact, I do)
and I am not sure if there is a special place to go to.
It's this world that has to be redeemed
and I think the dance the music the song the colours
must be visible
and I'm suspicious of this desire to be strong, be one.
Not sure that the weakness that is yours which I accept,
the weakness that is mine that you accept,
is not our strength, is not the source of love
and I think too
so much harm has been done to our tender parts,
so many of us have cultivated a bitter pseudo-strong
isolation
that to make love even when the hate comes boiling,
to be broken down in the struggle to reach another
is what the world needs now.
redemption of the body and resurrection of the erotic
child in our heart
so maybe what I'm saying is:
I will continue to be a poet,
to stay in the open, subject to all forces.
And I say this knowing I am damn near crushed at
the moment.
No, I choose that, I choose the fate of being here
amongst
all the shitty stinks of the streets and the hard nosed
bastards behind the wheels the levers the buttons
the handles.
Yes I choose that. I refuse to say the earth is not
mother

to all this, mother to all and many various and
conflicting
dreams deaths births nightmares beauties riots
confusions romances etc.

Yes maybe what I'm saying is I will continue to be a
poet,
one of the mascots of this area
rather than try to live religion,
I thank you for the invitation,
I was tempted;
And I hope it works out for you, pal,
Whatever that means these days.

*

we
  are in the hands
of
  something
that doesn't even
have
    hands

*

Quarried deep and fainted
Fell upon my face
Lay and lay and lay

*

– Why are they painting the ship, father?
– To enhance the beauty of the ocean floor, my child

SPEECH OF THE TYRANT, DEMOS

King: I am sword and order and terrible light.
Queen: I am hearth and fountain and terrible night.
King: I am founder, judge, and amnesty.
Queen: I am music, strife, and tapestry.
King: Without me the whole conception falls.
Queen: Without me the whole deception palls.
King: One glance from me and a man shall die.
Queen: One dance with me and a man shall cry.
King: Shall we go together into the hall,
To take our thrones and be seen by all,
And give those who wish it audience?
Queen: By all means, dear, the door is wide;
We shall enter as one, side by side.
King: And I shall stride.
Queen: And I shall glide.

And the courtiers bow deep to help them hide
The murder beneath obedience.

'What is that noise I hear in the street?'
– Treachery flounces on feigning feet.

'The people shout for you to appear'.
'That fearful noise?' – 'Is the poor man's cheer'.

The king mounts up to the balustrade,
Through silken hangings he has to wade,

But only once the herald has called out: 'Hark!',
When the feathered arrow finds its mark.

'Die, old tyrant! Long live the people!'
Cheers and bonfires, bells from the steeple.

But who in rags and which of the wretches
Can step forward now to speak of justice?

None. Centuries have seen to that.
Only one is ready to act.

Forward he steps to their high-clenched fist
And slips the chain of freedom round his wrist.

His men already speed through the land,
As he calls for silence with casual hand.

'Friends, I know how long you've waited this hour
That ends the plague of one man's power.

I, as you know, have long cherished the folk
And laid the plans that undid this yoke.

See beer and wine, meat and bread,
Are being laid out, and a crown per head.

And when you have eaten and when you have danced,
Rejoicing that this boil is lanced,

Return then home to village or city
And everywhere form a local committee

To discuss and discover what your will is
(Which should do your heads in, you incredible sillies).

I, meanwhile, will act as public trustee.
I'll keep it short now, I know you're thirsty.

And while you're debating (blind and blatant)
I'll be busy taking out patents

On marvellous inventions long suppressed
By the old regime's vested interest.

Aspirins, bingo 'n' coffee beans,
Rules of order 'n' duplicating machines,
Letters to the Editor 'n' televis-i-on screens:

So while I'm ruling on my owneo,
You can criticise all on the phone and by roneo;
Inflating your egos to such an extent,
You'll quite forget what all this meant.

Now: I want to hear cheers from all and from each
For these new freedoms: first, freedom of speech.

Freedom to gripe and freedom to groan,
To do whatever you want in your home;

To analyse all topics under the sun,
And go home from meetings one by one.

And I pledge this: no child in this nation
Will be allowed to escape from education.

And further: anyone suffering aberration
Will get entirely free incarceration,

Along with free application of the medical sciences,
Including the latest electrical appliances.

And if, despite this, you still feel neglected,
Every day you will see your opinions collected

In polls and surveys and in-depth studies:
Why, you and me'll be just like buddies.'

He waved once more, and stepped into the rear:
'Well, that didn't take long, did it, my dear?

Just a little under three hundred years
To wrap them up in invisible fears.'

And he frequently changes; indeed, he has no name.
No rulers now, chums: it's up to us to see through the game.

*

The king in his castle focuses upon the distant dragon
a beam of potent vision.
Deeper and deeper every day the dragon is pierced
as by a point of a ray of the sun
singled out and metalled
for one purpose only:

the knowledge known
as Victory

*

Sparkle, assassin, on my left.
Loom, unwanted, creatures to my right.
I go ahead,
And the wash from my nasal prow
Keeps you aback.

*

The devil! Why should I be afraid of him and his visits?
He's only a cultural element
Goddammit!
Yeah! And I am strong to give him room.
I am magnanimous, at least that's my middle name.
Let him pay court to me, offer his wares.
I can have a look, can't I,
And still kick him downstairs?
Sure, I can. Sure. Well, pretty sure.
And I do want to have a look.

WILD ONE

To know it we must name it
So I name it: fear
To know it we must name it

So I name it: love

between these two
the world is swung
and a man is hung
and there is nothing to choose
yes nothing
so I name it: nothing
and I choose it
yes choose it

oh don't go away
stay
please stay
I stand sole
in this hole
my dance has made
but not alone
grant me your
companion
ship
wild one, brave one
be
be afraid
and choose
be
unknown to yourself
I will know you:
by your flags
    your storms
    your waking eyes

THE ATTIC POEMS

1976–1977

You know that I was dead, don't you?
And there was nothing I could do
But be brave and practise discipline
Till I met you.

I COULD PANIC

I could panic, shiver, cry, abandon,
For what am I but fragile, slender,
Small, vulnerable, at the mercy?

But I do not (though I do sometimes).

No. I stand, I smile, I proceed
Precariously, but forward.
I stay in, though I love walking,
Love trees, air, conversation.
I stay in, where the pressure is on,
Simply because I too, in my small way,
Am a guardian,
And this work which burns me
Must be done.

WE ARE BEING BROKEN

We are being broken. I myself chose to be and, at the same time, could not avoid being broken.

I sat in my room like a motorbike fanatic with all the bits around me, and looked at them hopelessly, time and time again, or carried the bits around with me in my rucksack, yes the bits of the bike that was me.

Instead of travelling on it, I carried it for years, my broken self.

And I am not broken now
And I am not a Yamaha either or a Maharishi.

No, I'm home-slain home-born home-bred; here in the burning diabolical West where man is standing on the edge of nothingness – millions this time, hundreds of millions this time, not just a handful of mystics.

No, millions are being brought to the hard place whether they like it or not, because we are in process and time is full of meaning. There is work to be done and, ready or not, we have to face it. And the cities are the nutcrackers that will do the job.

Yes, that cracking noise you hear is marriages breaking. That weeping you hear is the unmarried mother alone with her child, that shouting you hear is the men in the pub getting smashed.

OPERATION

I am about to perform a surgical operation on the self.

*

There are no politics in this, there are no politics left in this, since I am not a mass man any more.

Politics being the mainly unconscious instruments of effecting what I can effect here in words:

the appearance on earth and into time of the giant forms that slumber in our minds.

*

The necessary suppression of dream to serve the
machine.
The rebellion.

The casualties.

ABOVE US, THE CLOUDS

Above us, the clouds, sun, moon, and the infinite
fucking starry night.
Below, the abyss.
Around us, the people, in varied stages of
disintegration and decomposition;
And still the assertion, still my fist is raised,
Though it holds yet no sword, though it has yet no
social purpose
In defiance of all non, all un, all black.
Be at one, we are told daily, we are recommended as
the way out of this impasse and deadly upshot.

Very well, sirs, of the loincloths of the ramifying
taboos, at one will I be. But since when has peace and
love been the whole story? Enough of this lopsided
trimming of the facts.

At one, maybe maybe not, but if so, why not with – avalanche, earthquake, forest fire, eruption?

The tiger lies down certainly, but with the lamb inside him; and that's when peace distils through's blood; that's when his love for the little lamb shines in his eyes – as his lids fall gently down to sleep. Eat drink and be merry – for tomorrow we eat another lamb.

Sniff it out, sniff it out everywhere, the lingering effects of the black-vested white collared enemies of the dance, the smashers of fiddles, the closers of the boozers; they're still there everywhere trying to tidy up the gigantic fact the universe is alive.

No, I am not a Christian. I am a raider from the North, a barbarian from the West, and the men I love are the men who die in battle.

Oh yes, when the black-red raiders come by night and set fire to your hallowed concepts, what then?

The wailing in the ruins? The moaning prayers raised towards the non-existent decomposed Father of the moon-rockets?

*

I'm on daytime alert and going on to: TOTAL CONFRONT

*

IBI

I've done it! I've did it!
Done exactly what I said –
Disconnected my head.
And you know what that makes me?
A man
A man with a destiny that can't be shakened off or questioned.
All I can do is weaken, all I can do is die.
Otherwise if I don't (and it's impossible now)
Then all I can do is *be*.
IBI
That's the name of the company, that's the name of the firm.
Sgonna make a lot of grammarians squirm.
'IBI is a global trading company, formed
to traffick in information between the
earth and the stars; and licensed to use
the only kind of instrument available
for this kind of work:
THE HUMAN BEAN'

I AM DIAMOND

I am diamond
I am indestructible diamond
Crushed into life by heat and pressure over years
In the dark underground
And I split the earth and came back up when I knew I was

Flawless sound

And I have red socks, and you must know what
that means,
Oh you who rummage in the lores of long-dead
cultures
hoping to find a clue from anything rather, anything
mother
anything father, than the you that's the world
that is you.

Oh I know you hope so to introduce
Eastern cults and practices
And the wisdom of the hunters of the moose.

No need to look so far
No need to leave the bar

This is the jungle mountain plain
You think you'd rather fancy to be shaped by
And the beasts are here – again.

Just shut your eyes and the phantoms will appear.

This is it
Can you take it?

This is it
Can you take it?

There is nowhere else to go
There really
Really?
Really!
Isn't.

HELL

Ah'm in hell ho
Ah'm in hell ho
Ah'm in hell ho
But Ah'm not fryin'

Ah'm the chief cook
Ah'm the chief cook
Ah'm the chief cook
An ah got here without dyin'

Just took a look
Ah wanted to see
Went underground
To reap victoreee

An the Maitre D' swished up to me,
Stuck out his paw and said:
'Glad you could make it, kid,
Musta bust your nails some,
Prisin' up that lid.'
I said: 'It did, it did.'
He said: 'Well here you start at the top
An work your way down.
You practise on others,
An you're allowed to clown.
Here's your hat an apron,
An I like ma coffee like ma women – brown'.

*

– And is it worth it, Mr Jackson?
– Oh aye, every bleeding minute.

BON VOYAGE

I want it to be clear that the I in this book is I.
I do not subscribe to any theory no matter how beautifully arrayed in religious verbiage.

I have read that I am that I am, and that is good enough for me.

Bon voyage, sombreros! We shall meet at some dawn or some dusk.

THE BEING OF BURDEN

I'm not into reason. I'm into creating a being of burden that can fly in the face of the gravity of the situation, that can accept these particulars viz:–

(1) Nothing is known
(2) Nothing is certain
(3) Nothing is coming your way
(4) Nothing's OK
(5) And nothing is nothing to get het up about.
It's nothing.

*

OUT OF THE RUBBLE

(spoken gravely and
slowly, with humour
in dark glances)

Out of dust disease and death
I rise to give my breath

Out of darkness difficulty and doubt
I rise with a great shout

Out of the rubble
One of the rabble speaks

I have become
the worst that I can be
And I have let the people see
Me
And so I am set free
To live between polarity
To enter into – hilarity

I am beyond judge law and reason
My only virtue is – to be in season

I have loved the mad the weak the oppressed
So long
Now I can only love the strong

You say there's only a few of us
Well
I was prepared to be the only one

If I have any pride

It's that I lived through –
My suicide.

Break on through to the other side
Break on through to the other side

I'm here because death said: Go.
Go back where it hurts
Where you have no place
Go – back to nothing
And make something out of it.

Not me speaking.
This is the forbidden voice,
The voice of the suppressed.
Be my guest.

We is not concerned with politiques
We is not concerned with statistiques
Is concerned wit people's concept of demselves
We is concerned wit what limits deir energy

We will play with fire
We will raise winds
We will sail through storms
We may even forget to take the boat
Like grass like fruit
Like coal and oil.
Like the lion's tiger's eagle's prey
I am here
                    to be consumed

*

BRIEF HISTORY

Brief history of human race: War!
Brief forecast of future of human race: War!

Zis is ze voice of your enemy
Zis is ze voice of ze people you fought
Zis is ze voice of ze persons you thought you had
destroyed
Zis is ze voice that will never go away
Zis is ze voice of ze under!
Zis is ze voice of ze other!
Zis is ze voice you luff to hate.
Zis is *your* voice.

Zis is ze voice zat everything sits on top of!
Ze whole fucking shitheap!
Ze members of parliament *und*!
Ze polizei *und*!
Ze magistrates *und*!
Ze ministers *und*!
Ze priests *und*!
Ze teachers *und*!
Ze two million laws on ze statute books *und*!
To control us *und*!
Ze burocracy *und*!
Ze social welfare *und!*
Ze psychiatrists *und* ze computers *und*!
Ze probation officers *und*!

Ziss is why they make the rules
Ziss is why they put us in the schools
This is why you carry the scars

This is why they put you behind bars
Because you are *wild*
Und! everything else *und*!
The controls *und*!
Because they do not want us to exist
Because they don't exist
And they don't know what it's a fuckin bout
And everyone that steps out of line they CHOP!

Just like dey chop de black man
An just like dey chop de primitive in Brazil
An just like dey chop de boy in school
Who is wild and proud and steps out of line
An dey chop him
But he keeps on going
But he has – the scars

Wear your scars
Be proud of your scars
But eventually grow out of them – pooh!

And vy zey look so dead on your screens?
Cos zey are ze voices of ze machines.
Zey are dried up. Zey are emptied. Zey are caput.

And we, we are de voice of de blood, of de earth,
of de dream,
Of de opposition, of life.
And zey will always try to smash us, to control us
Because they need us to run their machines
They need us to believe their lies.

*

DO NOT BE AFRAID

Do not be afraid of all this talk of blood
Do not be afraid of what de dry an dusty folk
declare
Of course de first time it come through, it come
through nasty
It come through rotten
It come from de bottom of de well
It come from de musty cellars
It come black it come slimy it come green it come
drippin
Old festooned cobwebbed spidered beetled fouled
But it come – into de air!
It release de poisons, it give off de stinks to de sun
And is de sun afraid of some stinks?
No!
It tell de truth.
Aaaah!
De troof!   Aaaah!   De troof!   Aaaah!

De controllers All de moralists All de ministers All de
fuckin slave priests
All de ones who tink dey know best
All de ones wid de goody goody pitchers
Dat sound too good to be true

Well, dat is right. Dey do sound too good to be true.
Dey is not true. Dey are liars.
Dey are liars against the blood.
Deir very rectitude creates disease
Deir clinical approach fosters illness
Deir mental rationality destroy de red cells.

Oh bustah, we're gointa have a lot of fun.
But dere sure as hell is
Gointa be a lot of trouble round dese parts.

THIS IS THE MESSAGE

OK RED BLACK   OK RED BLACK
Are you receiving me? Are you receiving me?
This is the message   This is the message
We're going over   We're going over
We're going to go through
They can see us but they don't know who we are
I think it's beautiful
Because what we're going to do is invisible
What we're going to do is Take our minds back
What we're gonna do is Believe in ourselves
What we're gonna do is Believe what we believe is true
What we're gonna do is Become invincible
What we're gonna do is Become

The person you attack in this war is yourself
They've got *their* hands inside *your* head
And you have to take your spirit and pull and burn
off the imprint
The imprint they made from the minute you were born
The imprint they made through home
The imprint they made through school
You've got to burn it out, you've got to dance it out
You've got to think your way through

It hurts, yes, it hurts,
And you stand the pain
And by standing the pain you become strong
And by burning out the message they put in
You make a space
Now, that space is nothing
At first it is nothing
And you are afraid of   nothing
I want to repeat that: you are afraid of   nothing!
There is nothing to be afraid of
Right?
There is nothing to be afraid of.
So
Having created that space
You are now ready – to receive
You have become a receiver
And by becoming a receiver equally at the same moment in time
You become a transmitter
And what you are a receiver of a transmitter of is
Energy
Yup energy
Which is fire which burns which they are afraid of

They, in a sense, are not our enemies.
No   They are our old selves   But
If they stand in the way of the spirit which is fresh and new
They must be defeated

Now   Listen to this   Listen to this
This is the message
They can't be defeated by force

They have the tanks they have the army they
have the police
They have the surveillance systems
But what they can't defeat, never defeat, is ones is tens
is hundreds is thousands
Of free spirits
And the purpose of this is clear
This civilisation is over
The new one the future can only begin in us
In one at a time, in one at a time
In a person, in a person
So: by rejecting the old by refusing to be told
You let yourself hear the new
You begin to allow the future to be born

The future is unknown
I don't know, you don't know, what it will be
But it wishes to be and, in order to be,
It breaks down people.
It breaks you down till you have no choice
Xcept: go on or die.

And oh yes, there are casualties, and oh yes,
there are suicides
And, oh yes, there are wars and broken marriages

We have to learn all over again how to live with
each other

Because this is a new situation
And nobody is afraid of anything but themselves
Their own energy their own amazing energy
Every one of us is amazing

Till we drank the drug of daytime sleep

And it has to be a war because that's how it is
Paradise is a dream
Peace is a dream
Of course we have peace now and again
But to want it is to dream (I mean personal, private,
you understand)

We are out of paradise.
We are here, we are at war, it is possible to die of
ignorance
We are conscious, it hurts

But – it's life on the planet evolving
It's life on the planet evolving
It's the mind going somewhere

And if you don't go with it, it may kill you
Millions of people have been killed in this
century already

DE SERMON

DE SERMON TONIGHT, BRUDDAHS AND SISTAHS,
IS ON DE TEXT: DE LOST POETS
IT IS UM SHORT TEXT FROM DE CHAPTAH
OF DE BIG BOOK OF DE WELT KNOWN AS:
DE FAUSTIAN MAN
DAT IS TO SAY WHEN INTERPRAHTED

DE REBEL MAN OB CHRISTENDOM
LET US TINK DEN BRUDDAHS OF DE LOSTNESS
OF DE LOST POETS
WHY IS DEY CALLIN DEMSELVES DE LOST POETS!
ID IS ONLY TOO EASY TO BELIEVE DAT DEY IS LOST
WHY DEN IS DEY SO BUSY TELLIN EBBRYBODY
DAT DEY IS LOST!
IS MEBBE DESE GADDERINS OF DE LOST POETS
LIKE DE MEETINS OF DE ALCOHOLICS ANONYMOUS
WHERE DEY MEET TO CONFESS? LIKE DIS:
BRUDDAHS AND POETIC SISTAHS
I USED TAE BE FOUND
I USED TAE BE IN ANTHOLOGIES
I USED TO DO UM READINGS IN DE SCHOOLS AT TWENTY QUID
UM SHOT
AND DEN I USED TO BE FOUND IN DE PUB
I HAB SAT BESIDE HUGH MACDIARMID AND CALLED HIM
'CHRIS'
I HAB DRUNK WID NORMAN AN REMEMBERED TWO
EPIGRAMS
I HAB CLIMBED DE SCOTT MONUMENT AN SEEN AS FAR AS
OXFORD
YEP I USED TO BE FOUND BRUDDAHS
I USED TO HAB OPINIONS
I USED TO . . .
AH BUT DIS IS BORIN
WHERE DEN IS DE LOST POETS LOST?
DEY IS LOST IN DE MIND DEY IS SOFT IN DE HEAD
DEY IS WEAK AT DE KNEES IN DE FACE OF DE TITANIC TASK
DEY IS HOWLIN IN DE MAZE COS DEIR WEE BITTIE STRING'S
GOT BROKE
DEY IS AMAZED TO FIND AFTER YEARS OF READING UM
MYTHOLOGIES

DAT DERE ACTUALLY IS A MONSTER IN DERE
DAT HAS DE BIG TEETH AND DE FLAMIN EYES AND DE
ARMOURED BODY
AND ONLY ONE VULNERABLE PART VICH YOU DON'T KNOW
AND YOU HAB ONLY TEN NINE EIGHT SEBBEN SIX FIVE
FOUR THREE TWO ONE SECONDS TO
AAAAAAAAAAHHHHHHHHHH FIND OUT!
DEY IS LOST, CHILLUN, AS EBERY MAN OB HONEST INTENSE
HUNS
MUST BE AT SOME TIMES LOST
DE POET DE PERSON MUST BE EMPTIED
MUST BE AT SOME STAGE AT DE MERCY
HE MUST LIE DOWN AND DE WORLD STAND OBER HIM
AND DEATH STAND OBER HIM WID DE POINT OF DE LONG
SHARP GLITTERIN KNIFE OF CHOICE FATE AND DESTINY AT HIS
JUGGLER VEIN
OH DEN: DE POETRY IS WEIGHED IN DE BALANCE
OH DEN IT COUNT WHAT SHOUT YOU SHOUT
WHAT SONG YOU SING
AH! DEN YOU LIVE! AH! DEN YOU KNOW!
DAT DEATH IS DE ONLY PROPAH COMPANION OB HONOUR
FOR WHERE IS DE LOST POETS LOST, SISTAHS AND BRUDDAHS?
IN DE BEAUTIFUL LARGE AN CAPACIOUS MIND
OB DE WORLD AH! DE MIND!
DE SUN DE MOON DE STARS DE EARTH
ALL CIRCULATIN IN DE MIND
DE WIND DE SEA DE VOLCANO DE DESERT
ALL FEATURES OB DE MIND
DE OAKS DE SWANS DE TURNIPS DE PEACHES
ALL GROWIN IN DE MIND
DE GUN DE BOMB DE CHOCOLATE BOX
ALL PICTURES IN DE MIND
DE LUBBLY LIDDLE KIDDYWINKS

DE FAT OLD DAMES
DE SMELLY OLD MEN
DE PIGFACE KILLAHS
ALL PERSONS OB YOUR MIND
OH OPEN OPEN OPEN OPEN UM UP
LET UM ALL BE
LET UM LIB WIDDOUT NAMES
DEN DAT WAY DIS WAY EBERY DAM WHICH
WAY
EBERY DAY DERE MIGHT BE
MORE PEOPLE AT DE DANCIN
YEAH, BRUDDAHS AN SISTAHS, WE MIGHT FIND
MORE PEOPLE AT DE DANCIN

THIS STORY

Awake!
I am the Cross
I conqueror destroyer seducer barbarian
I whom it has taken millenia to make and unmake
I, at this juncture of space and time,
One,
Alone,
Am
The Cross, the meeting place,
The flame floating in the heart of the bowl
The face peering in the mirror seeing not itself,
The sword and the stone,
The hero and the maiden,
This is I,
This story

This dream
Is all
I.

THE ONLY CONDITIONS

The West has been ferocious barbaric imperative
and consuming
I love the West
It has ransacked the world
It has destroyed simple people everywhere
It has emptied the world of meaning
Its wars have made nonsense of its religion
It has brought the world to the edge of destruction
It is blind one-sided materialist death-dealing
ignorant and vicious
And I love it
Because it is acting as the other hand of God:
It is closing every door but *the* door
It has mocked every truth but *the* truth
It is bringing the world to its knees
It is bringing humanity into degradation despair and
suffering
The only conditions out of which sleeping people
Can learn
To become

MASTERY OF FIRE

I am the spirit of the West
And I am fire

I am a prince of darkness and light
I am barbarico-sophistical
And beyond all measure, quick.

I am free:
To make me good you have to master me.
Otherwise I will turn you all,
The several hundred million of you,
Into an episode.

But to master me –
You have to be as awake as I,
As bright as I,
As mercurial as I.
To master me you have to love without reserve,
To master me you have to die;
To master me you must know more than earth
To master me you have to end the lie,
The lie there is no second birth,
And that tramping and trudging from till to till
is your worth.
Do you know that when you are seen you horrify
the spiritual eye?
That you have defiled every purity
And that only the gift of another who is not I
Has opened and made the way free for you –
My brother in heaven, Christ?

I am not his enemy, though it may seem,
I am as high as you can fly on your own
And that's
To death

THIS IS THE THIRD WORLD WAR

This is the Third World War
And we are the front-line:
The line vertically down our middle
And the line across at the height of our shoulders:
WE
        are crosses on our own graves:
Soldiers, victims, rapists, punks,
Nurses, reporters, casualties, widows,
Unmarried mothers, rebels, racists,
Delinquents, terrorists, bolshies, divorcees,
Of
THE THIRD WORLD WAR

Because we ceased to care for the world of matter,
Because we believed there was only the world of matter,
And that, therefore, what we did with it didn't matter;
Because we thought we were free, were grand, were flying,
And thought being free meant: no obligation;
Because we forgot WE are Adam to balance knowledge and tending,
Because we stamped on our conscience till its blessed voice

Became an ugly babble of ologies and isms,
A language of the intellect alone, whose deadness
and unusefulness
Is one of our greatest sins;
Because of all this, the social world, including:
All nations, states, classes, institutions, work and sex,
Are now subject to cataclysm,
That is to say, the sundering virtues of hate,
Which are issuing forth
In war, social struggle, terrorism, greed-demands,
Man-woman incompatability, sex-dissipation,
indulgent idleness
And attacks on and surrender of freedom.

The sundering virtues of hate lie in this:
Every *one* is being turned against every other *one*,
And so eventually back on *the one:*
The lonely frigidity of the self-mirrored self,
Until pain demands re-investigation,
The dusty records of the soul are opened,
The imprisoned voice of conscience released
And thought, real thought, not the debased
enumeration of artificial categories
Produced by anaemic inanimates,
But Thought, the glittering sword of discriminating
integrity
That loves
Will once more give shape and gleaming meaning
To our intercourse with that beauteous long-suffering
creature the earth.

UND MERCY

If you want me to tell you the truth, I will
but curse these old interests

hang on a mo, though

und mercy
for the child we return as

THE MAGICIAN AND THE DEVIL

It's the Magician and the Devil that meet here.

The one, our hero, to withstand the spells and illusions
the enemy surrounds and tempts him with.

And the Devil, in this case, left impotently to gnash his teeth
and shake fist in black-red fury, amongst his bevy of seductive ill-intentioned beauties.

And
apart, to the side, the Priestess waits to see, trusting,
praying for the youth, but waiting impartially the
outcome.

And what if the magician was defeated?
Would she, then, through compassion, go towards the wretch,
and, for a while lend him strength and faith?

Perhaps.

But this he must not count on.

*

Night closes in
On my lonely grin.
I wish I could remember
About narcissism again:
Is it or is it not a sin?

WHAT OTHER SHE THAN THOU?

Conscience stricken,
I hit back
And hurt my conscience badly.
Conscience stricken,
I raged 'Take that and that!'
It was so badly hurt now,
I couldn't stand the sight of it.
I stamped on it, the soggy mess
Of blood and tears.
'Look at you, look at you!', I cried,
'You snivelling heap!
Who are you to try and tell me anything?'
In my anger, I slipped and fell into the wretch

And her strong and beautiful arms
Came round me, said:
'Give in?'

A DOOR

–If it wasn't for me, what would you be?
–A twisted twig on a dying tree.

–If it wasn't for me, what would you have done?
–Howled on the ground and sucked my thumb.

–If it wasn't for me, what would you have seen?
–Drugs and thugs and hideous obscene.

–If it wasn't for me, what would you have known?
–Cruel minds, hard hearts, and a terrible throne.

–And who do you say that I am?
–You are my Lord, disguised as a dragon
You are my Lord, disguised as a thief
You are my Lord, disguised as murder
You are my Lord, disguised as grief

–And what do you call your loss?
–Justice.
–And what do you call your suffering?
–Fire.
–And what do you call your emptiness?
–Door. A door. A door.

NOW THAT I AM NOTHING

Custodian of the four ways
Guardian of the perimeters
Master of the centre
Heralds of the wind
Spokesman of the sea
Tribune of the square
Angel of the three sides
        Guard me now
        Build me now
        Watch me now
Now that there is nothing
Now that I know nothing
Now that I am nothing
Now that I am terribly afraid
Now that the structures concepts cities
Lie like windscreens in the laps of crazy drivers
And I struggle daily nightly every second
With fragment mind
Leering images
Riot imagination

Me with such a little knowledge
Such a little will
That only all I have
Is saying Yes

I TREMBLE AT THE DOOR

I wasn't brought up, I was dragged up
Bullied nagged and hounded
Into the slave shape of the time.
And when I blindly wriggled to be free,
I raved and ran amuck
Hurting many in my thrashing as I struggled with the chains.

Till, eventually, exhausted, I
Lay down and cried to consider what I'd been;
And would have still been there, whimpering,
Hadn't nothingness, like a blessing from hell,
Intervened.

Yes, my friends, confusion, terror and self-pity
Pressed me to become a man at last
And not a puppet rebel, with an:
Automatic Marxist
Automatic atheist
Automatic anarchist
Janov
Ron L. Hubbard
Maharishi
squeak

And now I tremble at the door,
I tremble at the door,
The time is now,
It isn't one or two or three or four.

I tremble at the door,
O help me, my friends, help me,
Or, at least, be there.

AGAINST ALL THAT IS DARK

I went on a journey to find who I am
I went very high so I could see the whole planet
I met the ones who weave and unweave
I fell apart and lay down weeping
I could not believe
I picked myself up and stood in my place
No one else stood there
There was no one by me
I was attacked
I was battered and beaten
I was picked up by forces
And hurtled around
I didn't like it
I didn't like them
I stopped and fought
        stopped and fought
        stopped and fought
Against all that was dark I fought
I that was nothing
I that was trembling
I that was weak
I fought
All abandoned, all undone,
All taken from me, defences, the usual,
Only one weapon,
Only one,
Against all that is dark,
Only one,
–The wish to love, to be one of,
To hold out my hand,
To smile on all,

Only that wish
Only that weapon
Against all that is dark
Only the tender, only the fragile,
Only the littlest thing in the world,
A spark, a child, myself, in the dark,
Only love,
Only even the wish, the choice,
To go in that direction;
Only a littlest tip of green.

With screams and curses,
Down went darknessess, one by one,
Down went empire,
Down went hugeness,
Down went images in succession,
Image after image,
Of self over and against an other,
Of self over and against any other,
Done through loneness,
Done through listening,
Done through the Word,
Which came through the words;
Done by the weakness of a child,
By nakedness and asking for help;
Done in the face of titanic entities
Who engulf and master and give false names,
Who, if you fight them, offer lordship,
Offer shares in ruling the dead,

Often I lay there,
Often pain,
But always a blessing when it's through.

I
praise the journey
praise the marker
praise the darkness
for its place.

I IMAGINED

I bit hard on knowledge
My teeth broke
My lips bled
I choked and gritted
My face went hard
I savaged my lovers
I despised freely
I was hammered by my blasphemies
Into abominable shapes
I ran riot
It became a disaster
I said I was a battlefield
I imagined I was a hero
I knew I was my enemy
I didn't expect to have to live with my corpse
I didn't expect to have to carry it with me
Explaining it to everyone
I didn't know it would become the dining room
For rotten maggots of fantasy, for
A thousand perilous yearnings seductively dressed
In all the fine colours of my own
Uncontrolled passionate energy.

But it is true, that if you can stand the pain
You can die die and die again
And guidance is given in every form
From coincidence to thunder.

*

Hard incredibly hard
 to be, and to aim
 and to fail
 and not blame
 and forget
 and begin again
 time after time
And to see that the worst
 was the most necessary part
 was in it from the start

*

From my window I see the rectangular blocks of man's
insolent mechanical ignorance rise, with hideous
exactitude,
against the sun
against the sky.
It is the University.

*

My friend, you told me I'd gained my knowledge
illegitimately
and it may be I know what you mean: but –
so severe is the situation

so much evil recently let loose
so demonic the mind and undernourished the heart,
great risks had to be taken,
casualties accepted
and sweet life itself
forced
to the point of death

*

I have no home
My boots are done
And tuppence in my pocket
And so I sing
Ting ling ling
My heart is in your locket

*

It's never like anything else –
The taste of birth into Time.

The rules are suspended – did you know that?
The old descriptions are only useful – a bit.

We are here with nothing but freedom
And our hearts – the sacrifice.

*

when you realise your freedom, you tremble
it is an awesome gift

a gift of titanic magnitude
to stand as an I on this planet
and be,
by virtue of divine consciousness,
a monarch;
free to abuse this,
to rend the delicate fronds
that convey confidence between living creatures
in any way I wish.
and the only corrective to this immortal power
that we, that I, as man, have
is the heart:
to feel pain, sorrow, regret,
to reach out a hand,
smile.

*

My path is clear
I must go on
Where wind and sun are fierce
Where the traveller throws his cloak away
And the landlord takes his tears
As he goes on past sights and sounds
Without a plan
Onto timeless ground
To make inner man
And helped by the love and teachings he sends
Meet the spirits of my friends
        And I don't know . . .
        How could I know

Since I've been locked up here
. . . .All I know is
        The name of Christ
And it's ending fear

*

My loves, if I had to leave you all,
it was to initiate the process
by which we can be healed,
those who wish to be healed.

We are sick, very sick;
We are unknown, very unknown;
We are lost, very lost;
We are hideously powerful.

each person must abandon as much as he can,
and so make room in his heart,
and suffer a space,
and allow for divine in-formation.

it begins by abandoning and (sometimes)
proceeds through uproar.

Consideration of flowers teaches one thing,
consideration of storms another.

Mercy is the name of this book.

It's the last thing anyone expects.

*

And from world I banished and banished
Until there was left just a
Little dripping me thing
That could only weep and crawl

And where did I drag myself?
– To you and to you.
And what did you do?
Fed me and clothed me, and listened;
Asked no questions, told no lies;
And never, never, no matter how I was
Flinched from looking in my eyes.

And I let you gaze cos I was not ashamed
To appear to you as an undone man.
We knew what we had to do
And were glad when it began.

HEART OF THE SUN

1978–1989

Just ahead of hunger's where I ride,
Below the rocks, above the tide.
Wind in my cape, star above,
We leap the debris and laugh for love.

THE COMPANY OF DOLPHINS

I am on a voyage of discovery
And those who are not are not just not,
It would seem, oh no,
They are by no means passive in their negativity,
I begin to gather, not a whit.

They would like to:
    Hole me hull
    'n' shiver me timbers.
    Spoil me vittles
    'n' chain me winds.

    Rupture me sails
    'n' frig me frigate.
    Mutiny me lads
    'n' spike me guns.

    Ruin me rum
    'n' jigger me compass.
    Blank me stars
    'n' banish me moon.

    Interfere with me sextant
    'n' stop me shore leave.
    Alert the patrols
    'n' have me up.

None of this can they do however,
Since all is invisible to them:
    Land I have left,
    Sea I traverse,

Wind that blows
And spirits that guide.

So ho –
In the meantime of their machinations
I'll fare without all such relations,
And, without a murmur, turn to enjoy:
The company of dolphins
The love of amphibians
And the conversation
Of the inhabitants of the ocean.

FRIEND

Dave
Where is Dave?
I don't know where Dave is
We don't know where Dave is
No one knows where Dave is
God knows where Dave is
His mother doesn't know where Dave is
And he's only twenty nine
Dave could be dead
After making some really giant effort to wake up
Worse, he could be lying low in England somewhere, signing on.

Dave went off to get himself together
None of us could help him
There was too much of him
He was all over the place

Hugely apart, magnificently undone
Generously strewn about the universe
I have no idea how Dave thought he was going to get
himself together
I suggested hard labour and keeping quiet for
two years
As a minimum approach
But I don't think these were high on Dave's list
somehow
No, I fancy he thought he could get away with it a
bit longer
I think he'll probably try out a few fancy ideas of
his own first:
Like founding a commune of hippies expert
in macramé
To weave him a huge butterfly net in which he could
be finally caught and bound
Or hiring pyramidologists to build him a shape
with movable walls
With an aperture at the top through which he could
pour himself
And when he was all inside filling the massy structure
to the brim
He'd shout 'Squeeze, boys, squeeze!' and the
hundreds of sweating men
Working in relays, backed by teams of maidens
bringing refreshments,
Would push Dave's periphery, that farflung
starhung glittering tenuous
Nebulous wild beautiful diaphanous skein of being
Towards his centre.
Ah if only, if only, what a diamond would the world
then have!

G

What a treasure!
What a golden flower would radiate us all!
But, amigos and amigessess, as you know only too well
And, no doubt, from bitter personal experience,
This is not how things are done on this
fascinating little ball
Of fiery mud we dwell on.
No, it's Trudge Trudge, I fear, only too often
No, I greatly fear, knowing Dave, as I do, like the
back of my hand
With which I must confess I often thought of
clouting him,
I fear, that Dave will not write to us till he can say:
I AM TOGETHER!
It could take years.
It could take lives

2

Oh Dave where are you? Dave I miss you. Dave I
loved you.
I mean love you.
I'm sorry I kicked your ass every day for a year
It hurt me to do it, Dave
Specially since you were always sitting on it
You sat on the government
And I had to kick it
You sat on your mother
And I had to kick her
You sat on your charm
And I had to kick that
You sat on your wit
I had to kick it

Dave, you were sitting on:–
Gurdjieff Kierkegaard Blavatsky Findhorn Jung Nietzsche Hesse
You sat on Castaneda
Like me Dave
Like me
Cos I was doing it too
That's why I can speak to you like this, Dave
Because I know you know this
I can speak to you like a brother
Because we are brothers
And particularly, Dave, you sat on your vision
You knew you had betrayed your vision
Like me, Dave
For it's hard isn't it to be embodied on this earth?
And it was easy in the sixties to disengage from the social connection
And fly for freedom in the face of the hard-working squares
And talk of being awake under the influence of substances and paperback books
But it's hard to come back, isn't it, and be grounded by gravity, still smiling,
Still with an open hand.
But it can be done
And has to be done
For it's hell to walk on earth with a vision of heaven
And not empty oneself of fantasy and let heaven be.
Yes, you sat on your vision of Jesus
You sat on your vision, Dave, and decayed visibly
Like me
Became fretted and frightened and subject to superstition

Like me
But generous to help me when I was at the end of my
own selfish fatal tether
You were the one to see and let me stay in your
flat rent-free
Try-ing-to-get-my-self-to-geth-er
And kicking your ass.
And we don't know where you are
But wherever you are
You're wanted Dave
I want to hear from you
I don't kick asses any more honestly
I neither need to nor want to or think it's much use
Dave, I want to hear from you
Whether you're together or not
Dave Martin, wherever you are, come in, come in
to the shore.

IST KAPUT!

'Sgone, all gone, it's over
everything that nearly everybody cares about and sees
is finished, over, doesn't work any more,
doesn't fit, is juiceless, a drag,
an interference, a dried-up blasphemy:
it's gone
the world of western material intellect
ist kaput!
thank God
and hooray for that!

*

I am as strong as I
Make way for angel
So how weak I have to have
The strength to be

*

love pours down on us all the time
from sun and stars and planets

Arthur's Seat is made of it
grass is green with it
I am drunk on it
Babes expect to be fed on it

Ah well, what they don't get from mater
They'll just have to get later:
        uncurl
        unfold
Turn their lead in for gold
And sing like birds in the gutter

*

God bless time and its operations
For indeed they are directional
And indeed the way is narrow
And comes to the point
Where the Cross is erected
And a person stands and says 'I'.

After the Confusion of Much
And the Desolation of Nowt

Looms the destination of One:
The Sun
The Son

*

We
we are terrible people
who've been called into freedom
to be failures
to be untogether
to pass through ignorance
to live without hope
to be unmarried mums
to be alone
to be subject to confusion
to have to think it all out for ourselves
in tears

*

who to live, had to bring into being
a world
a world which exactly fits and figures the other
the this the so-called external so-called real known
world
key to whose understanding of which
is called; Judge not.

*

I seem to have emptiness, grief, just now; but do I?
For within is pure intention
And absolute refusal

So what is this grief but a weather?
And what am I but an obedient earth?

*

I see you through the window of the night,
I see you turning round and round
Upon your dwindling pictures of yourself
And struggling to recreate every morning
False images to worship,
Based on your body, your
Fallible beauty, and your fear of death:
Because you wouldn't listen
I can only wait
And trust your suffering will be great enough
To bring you down, and stop your lies
With terror;
Since I know that only love can come
From abandonment
Honestly conducted.

*

How can I speak to you
  How can I reach
While you attach importance
  To anything mortal?

*

I had my last conversation
With . . . The World!
I shook my fist at it and swore

My last challenge to the Totality.

And, of course, it wasn't there –
Again;
Just you and me as always
Expressing ourselves
Perfectly imperfectly.

*

I keep asking for clarity.
Why don't I ask for charity?
Am I still afraid
Of being no one in particular,
Of being utterly unreal?

THE HAG

I saw the hag last night
A murderess,
Sucker of blood,
Cock bewitcher,
Very cruel and old and cares for nothing
But teeth and bones;
Ancient, indifferent, skiving and living
Off dreams of lust.
For she knows, if followed, they lead to her.

'Ah, my pretty ones, you think to indulge yourselves,
You think you can play, with fire, with love?

Well, you can, young sirs. Oh yes, young Romeos,
you can –
For a time.
But then you are here and here you stay,
A servant now of infamy and darkness,
Subject to the images
Of the mad cackling projectionist'.

OUR EARTHLY WEDDINGS

I took my thinking to the height of absurdity
And from there I was plunged to the depths of misery.
So I married my thought to the poor soul I found there
And she with her thanks has softened his fierceness
And he with his clearness has banished her mists
And she with her kindness has tempered his judgement
And he with his sterness has strengthened her purpose.
Oh that we should conduct our earthly weddings
so well!

*

I'm free to choose
  that's certain

not free to choose
what I have to choose
between

*

frail, yes
when I'm strong enough to be this frail
I can love myself

*

Slowly, tremblingly, out of the blue
A shape is made.

*

We are the Church, my friends.
Why do you think we met each other?
Do you think it was by accident?

Why do you think we circulate each other?
Feed console and amuse each other?
Love fight and curse one another?

It's because our stars constellate us
With our messages, gifts and debts.

Be one, and be one of the company.

'FREE'

I used to know so many fascinating things
ah my teeth were bright
my icicles white
I captured so much

between stalags might and tight
and where did it come from
but the library of night?
the laughter of prisoners
out on a spree:
on parole so long
they thought they were 'free'

*

In the gentleness of evening
I perambulate,
Led by father, sustained by mother,
Troubled by no one

What is this? The city.
What is that? The moon.

I never wanted much
And I never got it.

So see, how bright my spoon.

HERE I STAND

Do I stand? Yes I stand. Where?
Here where the wind blows.
Yes, where the wind blows. Here I stand.
The wind. I stand blows. Blows

It rains. It rains blows. I stand.

Do I stand? Yes, I stand. Where?
Here, where the wind blows, where it rains.
Where it rains blows, I stand. I stand blows.
I stand.

Why? Oh why ask why? Why not fly?
Yes, fly, to join me here, brothers and sisters,
Friends and relations, where I stand,
Rain or shine, where I stand
In the weather of the world.

Who? I.
Where? Here.
Why? Yes. Because I say Yes.

Oh sing all time tra li la
Me happy clear from top to toe
You didn't see me coming round the corner, did you?
I was in a pram.

ESTHER

I grieve without feeling, because I understand
That this I see must be, and I hold out my hand.

And if this is a picture of truth, could it be drawn
without wounds?

No.

Her way amongst men is hard.
She is bound to be scarred.
Yet I know her from long ago,
And she:
                    is a Child of Light.

THROUGH ALL DIMENSIONS

I am, through all dimensions,
Is

And earth
is all our names
most deeply spoken

FRIENDS

Friends of the mandolin, of the guitar and of the flute,
Friends of the open road and the jumble sale houses,
Friends of many talents, many possible careers,
Who preferred to hang out with each other, near
                    nothingness with the dog,
Until the message in the heart became clear.

Friends whose derangement was educational
And who put up with the intolerable in each other

Because we knew we were taking part in a process,
That something was being loosed,
And that none of us knew how to live with it,
Namely, our freedom.

Friends who knew that something was happening
because it was happening to them
And had the courage to believe and act on it even
when it looked and felt like failure
Friends who came in so suddenly from nowhere
at the right moment
That it began to be obvious that our spirits knew
what we were doing.
Friends who justified centuries of work loosening
the hold
Of the dogmatic and legalistic controllers of
information about the universe
When in one smile or joke or beam of the eye contain-
ing lifetimes of love and imagination and starlight
Years of loneliness etc. were washed away and once
again the staggering realisation came
That all that is necessary is to be Here and not
surrender
To the negative powers at present commanding earth
And indications of the next step will come in their
own good time

Friends to whose flat 'mad' people (I mean much
worse than us)
Were able to come and relax and have a cup of tea
and no one batted an eye
Because we too had been educated in rejection and
knew for sure that this – is a tough trip

Friends whose generosity of soul to the fallen
because they themselves were fallen
Revealed the mental hospitals etc. as prisons and
fear-pens run on behalf of sterile old consciousness

Friends whose use of poetry and myth as a means of
understanding life on earth
Helped to make many a dark night lighter and revived
the constellations in our hearts.
Friends whom I now understand prepared me to know
something of Christos, our companion in all these
matters.

Yes, friends of the mandolin and of the guitar and
of the flute,
Even after all these years I can't see for tears now
And what can I say but Thankyou for seeing me and
letting me know again
That I am one of the company on this voyage to
the stars.

YOU

from all the universe who came?
you
your hair your face your eyes
made from my heart
your fire your light your tragic coldness
arriving out of an intricately timed whirl
of people and events

so that we each had a friend in the world
when we'd reached somewhere no one else was
both of us orphans both rescued from death
what laughter we have because we are spirits
and what pain is coming! for I see
that you have no idea who you are in this time
and that you have forgiven no one.

*

I am the stranger at your door
and I'll keep on calling
till it is no more

*

Don't even think about it.
Persevere.

Naturally there are passages of opacity
Requiring tenacity.

*

Cease interpretation
Introduce action
and empty receptiveness

The soul that beautiful woman
long captive in her chair
is going to walk unaided
and for no reason

*

Is free now
Is free all over the world
Is possible
Is possible to die now and become
Is possible to rise from the old forms
Is possible to suffer this change
Is possible to become planet-human
Is possible
Is free now
Is free all over the world

THE WAY IS CLEAR

The world's being brought to oneness under the power of death
And yet the way is clear
The limited mental consciousness crumbles daily under the impact of evil
And yet the way is clear

The media, machinery and fantasy-fashion products enslave millions of minds
And yet the way is clear

Mechanistic legalistic materialist political and scientific concepts prevent understanding of humanity as a being among beings
And yet the way is clear

Old gods, and worse than old gods, are being revived because persons will not suffer the struggle of good

and evil in their hearts
And yet the way is clear

The world moves visibly towards titanic disaster
whether of fire or suffocation
And yet the way is clear

The rabbis priests and ministers still haunt their melancholy erections
And yet the way is clear

The artists take their gifts for granted and do not
acknowledge the angels they unconsciously receive
from
And yet the way is clear

The ritualists and fundamentalists revive their empty
forms, fill them with passion and are inevitably compelled to legislate and kill
And yet the way is clear

The masses define their meaning in relation to the
work-machine which is like manacling yourself to a
skeleton
And yet

the investigating spirits of the brothers and sisters who
accept love as their goal and so consciously take up
their destiny will not be defeated; and, through great
reaches of time, the earth, yes, will come to its
fulfillment resolution and transformation, for I have
seen that in the mind of Time

And the way is clear

HOME

You complain, do you?
About the difficulties, the lies, the hatred, the conditioning?
But they are your task, they are your material.
Without them, what would you be?
A cushion?
A lap-dog?
A brick?

It's your pain that stops you being inert.
It's lack of love that's driving you to think.
It's chaos that forces you to make a shape or perish.

Their cruelty was a knife to open you.
And, anyway, remember: they suffer from it themselves.

Without loneliness, you wouldn't learn that you are one.
Without loneliness not learn: a drop of kindness weighs the world.

You complain?

Are you the shoot that cannot drive through concrete?
Are you the seed can't grow on a ledge?
Are you the dog can't find its way home?
Over scores of miles?
Through rain, cold, hunger, noise, traffic, kicks?
Guided only by, yes, guided only by,
Guided by, yes, what?
By what?

Love, of course, you silly dumpling,
You snivelling, shivering wretch,
Guided only by love, and desire . . . . . .
To reach . . . . home.

And when there, oh, in whatever condition
You've managed to drag yourself there in –
Wet, filthy, starved, Belsen-ribbed,
  wanting nothing else but
        nothing else but
        nothing else but

There is . . . recognition, the quickening, the bark, the
        howl, the whimpering, and then . . . .
The door, the opening, light, the hands, the eyes, the
        voice
Of the one you love and went through hell to find
        again.

And from that one, what?
Yes, from that one, what?

Judgement? No.
Anger? No.

Welcome, immediately.
Embrace, immediately.

And so what your lostness?
  so what your misery?
  so what the years?
      the journey
      the loneliness
      the tears

the foulness
the faintings
the despair
so what, the whole bloody rag-bag of muck we
have to crawl through,
by love,
with love,
for love,
to love?
So what, my friend?
What
Were you complaining about,
Exactly,
Can you remember?

DOPE

The magician lurks in his cave
seeking to sustain himself
by ancient devices,
knowing all the time
that the world waits
the word
from the dancer,
the dancer
he sits on

The world leaps and paws, growls and hisses at
his door
(it seems)

but:

it is an imaginary world
seen from inside the cave
through the fumes of old torments
To die into the contemporary, the point of Time now,
to be raised, he is afraid, as we all are,
afraid to meet
the beings of the sun
the strong upholders of true earth
who bring us our future love

*

From A to Z is a long way,
A long hard way.
And what lies, think'ee, at the end of the alphabet?
Something even more difficult.
Chew on, my friend, chew on.

BARLINNIE*: THE WORLD

(slowly, in a Glasgow accent)

It's when ye start tae reach fer the stars,
Ye first find out ye're behind these bars.

Ye can't believe ye're caught in a cage,
An ye exhaust yerself in horrible rage.

*Barlinnie is a prison in Glasgow.

Ye think: 'What A need's more knowledge, eh?'
An ye read a' ye can get hud o' on bar-ology.

But the more ye read o bars an chains
Hammers disaster intae yer brains.

An then its plans an bombs an guns:
'If A can't be a man, A'll be like the Huns.'

But it doesnae work and ye begin tae sink,
An ye get so low ye begin tae think:

'A'll ask ma mates tae gie me a hand,'
But they're a' playin' games in the compound sand,

An watchin tellie an studyin' form.
'Aw c'mon,' ye say, 'this is not for what we wuz born.'

'What stars, what bars, what's up wi' you?
Whaddiye mean there's somethin tae do?'

An they begin tae ignore ye an tap their heids:
'He's queer him; when ye cut 'im, he bleeds.'

O.K. That's it. Screw them – rejection.
Put me down for the dejection section.

Maybe they're right tae sit on their asses,
Maybe the stars are just hot gasses.

'It'll a' be the same in a hundred years,'
Someone shouts as he wades through yer tears.

But ye don't gie a fuck, ye've closed yer folder;
An then ye feel this hand on yer shoulder,

An ye shake it off, an let out a curse:
'Lea' me alone, ye're just makin it worse.'

But he doesnae go, he sits down instead,
An ye hear these words comin intae yer head.

'C'mon, pal. Gie us a break. If you sulk alone,
That just leaves me out here on ma own.'

An for a moment ye're stuck, an tempted by night,
But ye've got tae look round, cos ye know he's right;

An when ye do, tae yer great surprise,
The stars, the furthest stars, are in his eyes.

CONUNDRUM

If I drop two oatcakes out of a fifth-floor window,
while waving goodbye to a gentle friend
who is on his way to India to find himself,
and at the same time trying to snatch a quick bite
before returning to my life's work entitled:
'How To Get On Top Without It Getting You
Down',

and

if one of the oatcakes falls into a sleeping baby's pram,
bashing its innocent nose to such an extent
that the nose bleeds and the baby yells

and

if the other oatcake should knock a kingsize into
the pram
from out of the hand of a passing
fourteen year old punk

and

if the mother who is up to her knees in dirty dishes
she using the old-fashioned method
rushes out to find the punk rummaging in the pram
for his lost solace while her baby cries
with a bleeding battered nose

and

if the said aggrieved and much careworn mum jumps
instantly
and forgiveably to the wrong conclusion
and yanks the punk by the hair meanwhile bawling
and shouting at him

and

if he, being a stranger both to the art of
articulate speech
and the legends of the Knights of the Round Table,
kicks her in the legs

and

if she, being immensely stronger and much angrier
than any young amateur of anarchism
drags him pell-mell round the corner to get justice

and

if meanwhile the wind, picking up a little, begins
to fan the smouldering Rothman's as it nestles
in the warm woollies of the howling babe

and

if also the plastic nappies of the babe are highly com-
bustible so that the rosy-cheeked one is soon the
centre
of a raging inferno and is with rather shocking speed
reduced to cinders, not to mention the pram and
it not paid for yet

well

I mean, am I to blame, am I to blame?
Myself, biased though I may be, I think not,
personally and without overly exercising myself,
I blame my friend who went off to India,
frankly.

*

Bon voyage, mes amis
We are in love
if only we knew it.

SALUTATIONS

I bring you salutations from the planets,
I bring you watch and welcome from the stars.
I come on embassy and with no weapons,
But with these gifts of words, ideas and symbols,
Traced from the stuff in which the high ones travel,
Transformed by medium and by distance,
By the ignorance of this small person,
Into shape-thoughts suitable for earth.

Through the barriers of death and dark
That are set about this dwelling place, I came.
Must please excuse the lateness of my speaking:
So fearful was the atmosphere I passed through,
So fierce the time and terrible my landing,
I was smashed out of the meaning of my visit;
And when murmurs of it slowly came to surface,
I'd been so shredded then compressed into a type,
I was staggered and disheartened by the chasm
Between what spoke within me and the day.

Then came my story like one of your long novels
Of which there is no need to speak here now.
I sum it up by saying: As I lay,
Listening to the message I had in me,
Repeating and rehearsing and comparing,
Alternately being weakened and made strong,
One came up very close and sat beside me,
Looked into my eyes and said: 'I see you,
And even if only I, it is enough.
Don't hesitate and don't mistake your meaning.
You are what your in-thoughts tell you, that is sure.

Stand up, go out, speak to those who listen.
Your embassy begins at every dawn.'

So my vehicle of travel was revived,
The robe of love and light that is my home.

2.

I bring you salutations from the planets,
I bring you watch and welcome from the stars,
When I remember I remind you we are spirits
Who can wake from death to life and lose our scars.

The word is clear, it is: to abandon.
The word is clear, it is: to suffer pain.
The word is clear, it is: to surrender.
The word is clear, it is: you are not lame.

I come from the realm of the creators
Who inhabit every molecule of space.
I look into this world which is still sleeping
And can only be unfolded through our race.

We do not know how rich we are with treasures,
We do not know what's done on our behalf.
We grind and cut up all the humble workers,
The trees, the herds, the whales, the little grass.

We try to cure our pains by public measures
Instead of turning to the heart that gives us breath.
Too proud to work beside the silent creatures:
What we legislate, en masse, is only death.

Yet what sleeps in earth and us will be awakened,
Like Arthur, and be sure, it comes through pain:
The necessity of hearts being broken open,
And the love that pours from who for love is slain.

I bring you salutations from the planets,
I bring you watch and welcome from the stars.
Be brave, all you who care for this endeavour,
We have yet to live and die through many wars.

HEART OF THE SUN

Long deep in the heart is the snake that illuminates
Further deeper than daylight intellect imagines
I went
I suffered the journey of darkness
The light of intention did not fail
I was havocked
I succumbed
I was spoken to
I rose

I am here now
As one of the brothers

I am here now
As one of the sisters

Here Now I Am
Not afraid of the evidence

A member of the heart of the sun

*

No wine in the fortress
  The grapes are in the field
And he who wants to drink with us
  Must raise the gates and yield.

The golden grains of love
  Lie scattered on the floor
Where does the trail begin?
  My friend, at your door.

NAKED IN THE WIND

Our civilization has reached (or passed) its highest peak – the point where it disintegrates as an externally impelled meaning vehicle and leaves us (apparently) facing space, alone. To think it out. To decide if we care. To become. To become who we are. You and me and . . . .

Oh horror. Oh death and damnation. Oh no.

But, oh yes, my brave ones, my lost ones, my comrades. For this is what we have thought for and fought for, here in the West, for centuries. The right to be free – of priests, lords, kings, squires, dogmas, systems.

Through all these and more, much more, the I of Western man has pierced till he stands naked in the wind.

Some laugh, some weep, some moan, some tremble, some legislate

There are drugs, political extremes, collections of beer-mats

Some to the cults, some to the groups, some to the East, some to the hills. Some reckon if we can only find out what Stonehenge was for, it will somehow help.

But wherever you run to, sinner man, de wind still blows, and calls your name.

Das is the situation, mes amis. It is as pure and fierce and cruel as the floe that sank the Titanic.

Love it.

*

gravely scarred
  who's this comes limping?

good   another friend
dragging their singleness
out of the hellish

*

Every sleeping earth-child has a friend.

CONTINUE

When the politicians, psychologists, physicists, or almost any public person now, speaks, we do not hear in their voices that they and we live on a teeming storm-world of thunder, rainbows, robins and Himalayas.

We do not hear in their voices pyramids or the chuckle of babes. We do not hear the Vikings, the Levellers, or Charlemagne or Krishna. We don't hear Christ or the good sound of wood as it splits.

Their voices have not been transformed by the facts of life on earth. There is no midnight in them, no dawn, no Venus. Yet without these and all the others, our thinking is only the re-arrangement of numerical dust.

What are we to do?

Continue with what we have always known we must: work towards becoming fluid beings alongside the angels of transformation.

*

Hunted, haunted,
I wasn't daunted.

What else was this
But what I'd wanted?

To stand against the wind.

*

I draw a circle round.
I raise triangle up.
To keep out every sound.
I have my dunce's cap.

*

The heart looked into the cloud that was its future, and saw:

crooked bent harsh speculations
corrupt visages
torn emblems of false virtue

It saw, and was stricken; and so, by the courtesy of reverse inspiration, breathing slowly, with back straight, and head very slightly nodded in acknowledgement, it went forward into the disastrous landscape, singing softly; invisibly lightened by the company of good spirits.

And a ray of sun; and a bird sang; and a hedgehog grinned and the gaffers waved, and the calamities gathered to meet what they cannot defeat: a human heart in Christos.

*

Old friend, the reason I came to lie bleeding on your doorstep is because in any other form you would not have accepted speech from me.

But because you allowed yourself to be touched by the suffering human form, not knowing it was me, I was able despite the prevailing earth-conditions of illusion to direct certain thoughts to your heart; and both our angels rejoiced.

And I? I was grateful, for my wounds were real. As real as yours that called me.

*

The love in the heart of a stranger
  That you have yet to meet,
The love in the heart of that lost one
  Has begun to beat.

But she does not know it is love
  To her it is a dream
That bends her day out of shape
  And makes her scream

For the stranger must start walking,
  Must wear out every shoe;
That lost one has begun to die
  To bring her love to you.

*

of such a flower
the children are shaken
because nobody speaks
of such a flower
  as actually is
their hearts are crumpled
because nobody speaks

of such a flower
  as actually is

because nobody speaks
of such a flower
  as actually is
their eyes become vacant
dull hatred begins
to penetrate their limbs
because nobody speaks
of such a flower
  as actually is

the children

THE IMMORTAL

Someone with great confidence can set out
from the other side of the world to find me
that if I was not here I would not think
of travelling.

Neither of us knows that the other exists.
But we will meet outside a boutique
and go for coffee

and between laughter and trembling amazement
the hemispheres will open and a child will be born

    love will smile
    we will hear from the stars

our angels will be able
to breathe better into earth

and we will be perplexed and enriched by troubles
beyond anything we have ever heard of;
moody hate will force us to think
how on earth to conduct ourselves
through the barbarity of the unredeemed
that we bring out in each other;
sweet freedom and difficult duty will tear us
till we grip both the reins, she hers, I mine,
with such intensity of purpose
that the planet appears as all-souls,
the immortal establishes itself between the heart
and the brow
and we learn to wear earth as it should be worn –
as the last work of the gods
before Love.

*